# Zen
## and the Art of
# Appreciative Inquiry

A glass half full approach to organisational development

Roger Rowett

Copyright © 2012 Roger Rowett

First published in 2013 by Amazon.

All rights reserved. No part of this book may be reprinted or reproduced or utilised in any form or by any electronic, mechanical, or other means, now known or hereafter invented, including photocopying and recording, or in any information storage or retrieval system, without permission in writing from the author.

Note – the author is generally open to his original content being reproduced with permission and suitable acknowledgement. Roger can be contacted at rogerrowett@btinternet.com ☺

All rights reserved.

ISBN-13: 978-1482647259

# DEDICATION

To Becky and Ceri – be curious, be interested in things,
and be open to new ways of seeing the world.

# CONTENTS

|     | Acknowledgments | vii |
| --- | --- | --- |
|     | Foreword | 1 |
| 1 | Introduction | 3 |
| 2 | My Discoveries | 8 |
| 3 | Appreciative Inquiry – the theory | 34 |
| 4 | The application of AI – the 5D cycle | 51 |
|   | Define | 54 |
|   | Discover | 62 |
|   | Dream | 67 |
|   | Design | 75 |
|   | Deliver | 84 |
| 5 | Does it work? | 89 |
| 6 | Doing it well – key elements | 98 |
| 7 | Measuring success | 101 |
| 8 | How AI can be applied | 108 |
| 9 | Five scenarios | 115 |
| 10 | What next? | 132 |
| 11 | And finally… where is all the Zen then? | 139 |

# ACKNOWLEDGMENTS

There are many people who have contributed to this book, both directly and indirectly – I would like to acknowledge a few of them.

To Jo for setting me off on my AI journey.

To Mette, Jane and Christine for giving me so many of my AI jigsaw pieces.

To Neil for helping me bring AI to Wales.

To Gill, Alison, Julie, Mark, Peter, Nadine and Rob for the invaluable feedback on my early drafts.

To the Italy Gallese crew for being the inspiration to DO IT and for the wonderful silences.

*The application of this knife, the division of the world into parts and the building of this structure is something everybody does. All the time we are aware of millions of things around us - these changing shapes, these burning hills, the sound of the engine, the feel of the throttle, each rock and weed and fence post and piece of debris beside the road - aware of these things but not really conscious of them unless there is something unusual or unless they reflect something we are predisposed to see.*

*We could not possibly be conscious of these things and remember all of them because our mind would be so full of useless details we would be unable to think. From all this awareness we must select, and what we select and call consciousness is never the same as the awareness because the process of selection mutates it. We take a handful of sand from the endless landscape of awareness around us and call that handful of sand the world.*

*Once we have the handful of sand, the world of which we are conscious, a process of discrimination goes to work on it. This is the knife. We divide the sand into parts. This and that. Here and there. Black and white. Now and then. The discrimination of the conscious universe into parts.*

*Robert M Pirsig – Zen and the Art of Motorcycle Maintenance*

# FOREWORD

Those of us working across the domain of organisational development who have occasionally flirted with Appreciative Inquiry as a change technology, will immediately see the value of this book. It captures the essence of engaging and transforming the way we think and act and reminds us of the most important ingredient in delivering organisational change – people.

For those who perhaps, have little knowledge or experience of Appreciative Inquiry, but a keen interest in expanding their personal and professional horizons to discover new ways of delivering change – this book provides a solid platform for beginning the journey.

As a description of the Appreciative Inquiry process, it offers an intuitive and experiential account of how to engineer change in an engaging and liberating way. It provides a solid evidence base for re-thinking the approach we take when working with organisations to transform practice. But more than this, Roger Rowett introduces us to a different way of understanding the world beyond the application of a set of principles and procedures.

In a warm and self-deprecating way, he convinces us that to fully understand and engage with the idea of Appreciative Inquiry we have to recognise the sanctity of relationship and the ocean of human potential that exists in everyone. In this regard, Appreciative Inquiry is an invitation to see the world in a different way, to re-construct the social and to acknowledge the connectivity of all things. We are reminded clearly that without exception, everything is delivered through relationship.

Often in our desire to deliver change we focus upon the transactional, believing that small practical steps exchanged in the moment will lead to transformational outcomes. This is rarely the case. In fact, I am unable to recall a credible example of where this has occurred in the world of organisational development. 'Zen and the Art of Appreciative Inquiry' provides a template for making the art of the possible probable and for delivering breath-taking change through people.

In the current climate, the certainty we once felt about what we do and how we do it has eroded considerably and we are left vulnerable to the fear that we may not be able to provide the solution or answer to the problems we face. Rowett portrays Appreciative Inquiry as a strengths builder, enabling us to tap into a positive core that holds the potential for achieving

## Foreword

immediate and long term success and for stepping towards the future with courage. Sharing his discoveries, will help to build confidence in using Appreciative Inquiry and trusting the process to yield unimagined benefits.

Some years ago, I was involved in helping an organisation to set a new course on its journey towards delivering world class healthcare. It wanted to radically reshape the way services were delivered based upon a new approach to working collaboratively with other delivery organisations, patients and the wider community. Using Appreciative Inquiry, to divine the future, 300 key stakeholders, some of whom were highly critical of the organisation with long established stories of contempt and criticism were brought together.

The process was underpinned by the principles and practices detailed within this book. To my surprise, the outcome was transformational. Those who came to the workshop with long held grievances and ritualised distrust let go of their discontent and doubt, those who came with cynicism and disbelief rekindled their sense of hope that a new way could be found and those who came to be heard who already knew where the future lay were listened to. Everyone left feeling fulfilled, part of a greater good and confident of their future role in delivering a new way forward.

Read this book when you need to recover your sense of mission and priority, read this book when you need to revisit the truths that connect us all as human beings and read this book when you want to explore an alternative way of delivering a better future.

Dr Neil Wooding
Director, Public Service Management Wales

# 1. INTRODUCTION

Just one question – when you have been involved in training that sought to change behaviours or culture; or been involved in general organisational development activity, do you think it made a real difference?

When you look at yourself and the other people involved, has it had a transformational effect in any sort of sustained way? Has it engaged and impacted on those individuals or teams who really needed to be 'moved' out of their comfort zones into new ways of thinking and behaving?

> *"Quality is what you see out of the corner of your eye"*
>
> *Zen and the Art of Motorcycle Maintenance*

This book is about a powerful approach to organisational and individual development called Appreciative Inquiry (often just referred to as AI). It lays out, in simple and straightforward language, the thinking behind Appreciative Inquiry and how it can be applied in practice. It is for individuals and organisations.

The book proposes that much of the developmental activity we carry out at an individual, group and organisational level has minimal impact. This is on the basis that we often fail to engage people in terms of where they are 'at' in relation to their own development and understanding - their 'map' of the world. The result of this is that many people do not take real ownership of action plans at any level. If this is true (and this is often my experience), this has significant implications for the way we train and develop people.

Within organisations this book is particularly for managers and anyone who has responsibility for developing individual staff or the broader organisation. It is also highly relevant to HR professionals who are seeking to support the workforce to develop and be most effective in their roles.

In relation to individuals, employed or not, the book provides a series of challenges to the way we (you) normally think about life and our part in it. How we develop as people. How we learn. How we see and hear. How we relate. What influences us and how.

The book itself has many influences, key amongst these is the cult novel by Robert Pirsig - Zen and the Art of Motorcycle Maintenance. I have read this book three times at different points in my life and each time discovered new learnings. The most recent was actually after an eventful motorbike trip from Wales to Italy for a training course.

Pirsig stated at the beginning of his book – 'what follows is based on actual occurrences... it must be regarded in its essence as fact. However, it should in no way be associated with that great body of factual information relating to Zen Buddhist practice!'

Similarly, this book is based on actual occurrences – my life. Similarly, in no way does it profess to convey that deep body of knowledge and understanding that is Zen!

Appreciative Inquiry grew out of a doctoral program in Organisational Behaviour at Case Western Reserve University in the United States in 1980. It was the result of a collaboration between David Cooperrider and Suresh Srivastva. It is still relatively unknown, but is increasingly being used by organisations to engage with key stakeholders in order to improve and develop. These organisations are as diverse as the US Navy, UK retail chain Halfords and Britain's NHS. It is also being embedded within some management training programmes.

> *"Of the value traps, the most widespread and pernicious is value rigidity. This is an inability to revalue what one sees because of commitment to previous values. In motorcycle maintenance, you must rediscover what you do as you go. Rigid values makes this impossible"*
>
> Zen and the Art of Motorcycle Maintenance

At the point of writing this book a news story broke (Oct. 2012) reporting that the Founder of Green Mountain Coffee Roasters (Robert P. Stiller) had given $10 million to Champlain College School of Business in the United States. The story stated that Stiller wanted to improve business education with many of the tools he used to empower, develop and engage the people in the two successful companies he built. Champlain College president said that "Robert Stiller built Green Mountain Coffee Roasters into one of the most financially successful companies of the past 25 years, embracing and leading business in making the world a better place with its focus on social responsibility and by providing a great place to work. A key aspect of their management practice was incorporating Appreciative Inquiry techniques". This is one of the many examples of highly successful companies recognising the benefits of Appreciative Inquiry and the potential it has to drive business improvement.

At one level this book attempts to provide a clear and simple overview of the thinking that underpins Appreciative Inquiry and the most commonly used methodology for delivery – the 5D cycle. However, it is also a personal account of the journey and discoveries that led me to embrace this way of thinking and working. It aims to develop your understanding of why the process is effective at an individual and organisational level. Like any theory, the critical learning will take place when you apply it, but I hope the book will support you in your own journey of discovery, in putting your pieces of your own personal jigsaw together.

> *"The truth knocks on the door and you say - go away I'm looking for the truth"*
>
> *Zen and the Art of Motorcycle Maintenance*

The book also attempts to explore the Appreciative Inquiry process at another level, looking at the essence of appreciation and what that means in a holistic sense. It will hopefully extend and challenge the way you think about and interact within your world – whatever that world is. It recognises the uniqueness within us all, whilst also sharing ideas about what makes us the same and part of one whole system.

Wujin Chang, a nun, asked the Sixth Zen patriarch, Hui Neng, for help in understanding the Mahanirvana Sutra. The master answered that he could not read, but if the nun would read it aloud for him, he would do his best to help her.

The nun then asked, "If you can't even read the words, how can you understand the truth behind them?"

"Truth and words are unrelated. Truth can be compared to the moon," answered Hui Neng, pointing to the moon with his finger, "And words can be compared to a finger. I can use my finger to point out the moon, but my finger is not the moon, and you don't need my finger in order to be able to see the moon".

This book is not the moon, it is just one finger pointing at the moon.

Introduction

Finally – you will see that this book is littered with quotes from other sources, they may seem random and at times totally irrelevant or 'off the wall'. Just read them and absorb them. They may mean something, they may not, but that's fine!

*What you have to do, if you get caught in this gumption trap called rigidity is slow down - you're going to have to slow down anyway whether you want to or not - but slow down deliberately and go over ground that you have been over before to see if the things you thought were important were really important and to... well ... just stare at the machine. There's nothing wrong with that. Just live with it for a while. Watch it the way you watch a line when fishing and before long, as sure as you live, you'll get a little nibble, a little fact asking in a timid, humble way if you're interested in it. That's the way the world keeps on happening. Be interested in it.*

*Robert M Pirsig – Zen and the Art of Motorcycle Maintenance*

## 2. MY DISCOVERIES

When I was young I read 'Zen and the Art of Motorcycle Maintenance' by Robert M. Pirsig (for the first time). It was one of a number of experiences that had a real impact on my life. It helped that I was 'into' motorbikes from an early age. I guess it also helped that I had a fascination with Eastern thinking, prompted to a great degree by the death of my father when I was in my late teens. One of those classic 'what IS really important' moments.

Throughout my life I have had pivotal moments of learning, experiences that have had real meaning and resonance. I have also been influenced by particular people, some I have known, others I have not. This book includes reference to some of those, including the work of Carl Rogers (often referred to as the 'father' of counselling); Eastern thinking and philosophy; Aikido; and of course last but not least – my Appreciative Inquiry journey.

It is at this point that I should probably quote Hitch Hikers Guide to the Galaxy and say 'DON'T PANIC', especially if you consider yourself a reasonably rational HR manager of a large corporation. Let me assure you that this book has its foundations in logical thought and a process that has a substantial history. It puts my learning into context. It attempts to share with you my evolving discoveries of little bits of life's jigsaw (and more about that later) in the hope that some of this may resonate with your own learning. This is on the basis that we all have times in our lives when the 'time is right', when we just seem ready for that next stage of understanding that could not have occurred at any other time.

The commonly used methodology for the application of Appreciative

Inquiry is called the 5D cycle (Define, Discover, Dream, Design and Deliver). Later in this book I will explain this in full.

The Discovery phase of the cycle involves a process whereby participants share experiences that had some deep level of meaning. This is based around a theme that people 'Define' in the first phase of the process (the first D). Participants then explore what contributed to that experience - what gave it life and meaning.

In this section I am going to share stories with you about my personal moments of learning and what gave them life and meaning. These will then hopefully underpin and complement the theories and principles behind Appreciative Inquiry that give it meaning.

These are five personal discoveries that have contributed to my understanding of how people and organisations develop and improve. They have unfolded throughout my life, and, I will propose, in a timely manner.

These discoveries are important to me because I experienced them. I hope they will resonate with you, but in one sense this does not matter. If you agree that what actually matters to YOU is what YOU have experienced, not what I have experienced, my point will be made. If you do actually connect with some or much of what I am saying – that is icing on the proverbial cake.

These personal discoveries are not in any order, either in terms of importance or chronology; they are all important in terms of my understanding of how and why Appreciative Inquiry works. Possibly, if I had not had these experiences and thoughts Appreciative Inquiry would have totally passed me by and I would not have written this book. I guess it is all about "Sliding Doors" – an excellent film if you haven't seen it.

## Discovery 1 – A glass half full

As I was carrying out an edit of this section of the book I checked the mail at the front door. There were no letters, but we did have two leaflets from local Jehovah's Witnesses. One caught my eye, it said – 'Would you like to wake up every morning with happy, positive thoughts?'. It then went on to say 'that's exactly what the Bible promises us for our future'.

Sadly I am not religious, spiritual yes, religious no. I say sadly, because I have often envied people who have a passionate and unerring belief in a God that will save us and make everything right and well in the world. And I often think, even if they are wrong (i.e. there is no God) and I am right, who is better off if quality of life is measured by levels of happiness and contentment? Of course, that's ignoring all those church attendees who get told week after week that they are sinners and require constant forgiveness!

> *"We were both looking at the same thing, talking about the same thing, except he was looking, seeing, talking and thinking, from a completely different dimension"*
>
> *Zen and the Art of Motorcycle Maintenance*

Rather than being at the whim of the gods (or God), I have always believed that we all have the power to influence much more of our lives than we think. Often it can feel that we have little control of the events around us (and the emotions that we associate with them), but in many cases it is our view of those events that have the greatest impact on our lives rather than the events themselves.

When we complain that we had a bad day and feel dejected, we usually describe external factors that were the cause of the bad day. Maybe we lost a contract in work or did not finish off a report in time, maybe we had an argument at home with our partner. Actually, what occurred here is that it was our interpretation of these events that made us feel the way we did. The fact is, two people can view these same events in totally different ways, one seeing the negative aspects of losing that contract, and another seeing this as an opportunity to learn and improve the next time.

The critical importance of how we view our world, how we interpret what goes on around us, has been written about by many people. Possibly one of the most well known was Martin Seligman.

Martin E.P. Seligman, Ph.D is (at the time of writing) the Director of the Positive Psychology Center at the University of Pennsylvania and one of the leading proponents of positive psychology. His work builds on that of Aaron T. Beck and others. He is the recipient of two Distinguished Scientific Contribution awards from the American Psychological Association, together with many other awards and accolades.

After 25 years of study Seligman proposed that the defining characteristic of pessimists is that they tend to believe bad events will last a long time, will undermine everything they do, and are their own fault. The optimists, who are faced with the same events, think about their situation in a different way. They tend to believe defeat is just a temporary setback, that its causes are confined to this one case, and that defeat is not their fault.

These ways of thinking are generally habitual and Seligman says that hundreds of studies show that 'pessimists give up more easily and get depressed more often'. The same studies show that optimists 'do much better at school and college, at work and on the playing field'.

Specific therapies have grown out of these theories, one of the most high profile being Cognitive Behavioural Therapy (CBT). These therapies seek to change and challenge individual's belief systems in order that they see things in a different way.

> "Enthusiasm is the yeast that makes your hopes shine to the stars. Enthusiasm is the sparkle in your eyes, the swing in your gait. The grip of your hand, the irresistible surge of will and energy to execute your ideas"
>
> Henry Ford

Apart from Seligman, many other people have conducted research into positive affect. One other I will quote is one of the papers of Sigal G. Barsade and Donald E. Gibson called 'Why Does Affect Matter in Organizations?'. Barsade is an Associate Professor of Management at the Wharton School, The University of Pennsylvania. Donald E. Gibson is an Associate Professor of Management at the Dolan School of Business, Fairfield University.

This paper reviews what we know about 'affect'. This is an umbrella term encompassing a broad range of feelings that individuals experience, including feeling states which are in-the-moment short-term affective experiences, and feeling traits which are more stable tendencies to feel and act in certain ways. In organisations this relates to focusing on how employees' moods, emotions, and dispositional affect influence critical organisational outcomes such as job performance, decision making, creativity, turnover, teamwork, negotiation and leadership.

The paper covers a wide range of fascinating discoveries about the way we operate as individuals and organisations including phenomena such as 'emotional contagion'. The paper describes this as a 'primary mechanism through which emotions are shared and become social, creating collective emotion'.

The work of Lyubomirsky, King, & Diener (2005) is quoted in relation to a comprehensive meta-analysis indicating that an individual's tendency to experience positive emotions and moods is associated with increases in a variety of work performance measures, including more positive supervisory evaluations, higher income, enhanced negotiating ability, and performing discretionary acts for the benefit of the organisation.

> *"There is no such thing as a problem without a gift for you in its hands.*
>
> *You seek problems Because you need their gifts"*
>
> *Illusions by Richard Bach*

The paper goes on to talk about how positive affect can influence a whole range of organisational variables including higher income levels, improved decision making, more flexible and creative thinking, and lower turnover and absence.

Finally let me give you one example of a person who was able to transform his life through changing his perspective; a man called Richard McCann. I was fortunate enough to hear Richard speaking at a conference last year and he was probably the most inspirational speaker I have ever heard. He was inspirational for a number of reasons, but most importantly because he was not just talking about a theory, he was talking about his own life.

Richard is now in his forties but at the age of five he woke up to discover that his mother had disappeared. She was the first victim of the notorious Yorkshire Ripper, Peter Sutcliffe. Richard's life from that time on was like reading a textbook on a lost childhood. He was exposed to drugs, abuse, suicidal thoughts, deprivation and pain – right through into his adult life. When he was talking, Richard spoke about the influence one adult had on his life, one person who said that he could get through this – and he did. He did it by a belief that he could do it – that he could change his life. This is just a short summary of an amazing person with an amazing story, but if anything can demonstrate how powerful the mind can be this is it.

I am not suggesting most of us are like Richard McCann. Probably none of us will go through the sorts of events that Richard experienced, and probably few of us could have had the strength of mind to get through them in the way he did – totally turning his life around. But the principle is the same whoever we are.

I will certainly speak for myself here. I have had a few knocks in my life (parents divorcing, father dying when I was young etc.), but nothing like Richard's. Of more relevance to this book - although I know this 'mind stuff' is true, I am often not good at doing it. What I mean by this is that I know for sure it is the way that I think about events in my life that affects my moods and emotions. I know that if I interpret them differently (generally more positively) I can improve my levels of happiness – and probably health. But… can I do it all the time – no.

> *"Every person,*
> *all the events of your life*
> *are there because you have*
> *drawn them there.*
>
> *What you choose*
> *to do with them is*
> *up to you"*
>
> *Illusions by Richard Bach*

The fact is this 'mind stuff' isn't easy. Conceptually it is – all I have to do is think differently – how difficult can that be? In practice it is very hard.

So I am going to leave the sales job there. All I am trying to convey is my total belief that we are the referees in our own game of life. If we really want to change our life we just change the referee! There is one more factor in this equation that I have not even touched on here, and that relates to the core principle of Appreciative Inquiry – social constructionism, but more on that later!

## Discovery 2 – The work of Carl Rogers

This book is primarily about organisational development and improvement, but let's not forget that organisations are made up of individuals. On this basis an understanding of how individuals develop, communicate and respond to each other has to be of some significance in relation to how effectively organisations operate.

When I worked within the care and education inspectorates, I often had to respond to situations where organisations were perceived as failing in some way. Within the care sector we operated what was often referred to as a RICE process – registration, inspection, complaints and enforcement. Organisations could fail at all these stages. They could fail to meet the required standards to operate at the outset, registration. They could fail on inspection, highlighted by an inspection report and associated requirements and recommendations. Or they could fail so badly that they had legal notices served on them, ultimately having their registration withdrawn, resulting in total business failure.

> *"Optimism is invaluable for the meaningful life. With a firm belief in a positive future you can throw yourself into the service of that which is larger than you are"*
>
> Martin Seligman

All this was about the organisation as an entity, but where there is organisational failure there is individual failure. These might be isolated incidents, or more usually systemic issues that had developed over time. But either way, all these issues arose out of something that could be tracked back to how individuals acted and related to each other.

> *"The real voyage of discovery consists not in seeking new landscapes, but in having new eyes"*
>
> Marcel Proust

To provide an example, usually complaints came to the care standards inspectorate when they had spiralled out of control, when people (the complainant) had become so frustrated with the situation that they contacted us. When you investigate a complaint you track the problem back. As far as you can, you look at the origins, the seeds of the issue that has now escalated to this level. When I say 'this level', sometimes this was pretty serious stuff like people dying – can't get much more serious than that!

A common factor throughout most (if not all) the incidents was some level of communication breakdown. And that communication breakdown was mostly due to breakdowns in relationships between people. Conversely, I should also add, that when organisations work well, it is mostly due to the same thing, except in this case the nature of the relationships support effective communication.

So what is it about us as individuals and how we develop that is pertinent to how we operate within groups? What is it we need to understand in order to support individuals to operate most effectively and contribute to group or organisational excellence? Let me tell you what someone called Carl Rogers proposes about this.

> *"Set me a task in which I can put something of my very self, and it is a task no longer; it is joy; it is art"*
>
> Bliss Carman

I first discovered the work of Rogers when I was in my 20s. I was working as a youth worker for the YMCA and was fortunate enough to be supported to attend a number of Counselling courses. I have to say that I struggled with what I perceived as Rogers' simplistic view about the power of listening and reflection (the essence of his work).

Over the years, many people had (and have) used Rogers as a foundation of their work and 'moved on' to more interpretive methods of counselling and psychotherapy. However, Rogers' simple messages have kept coming back to me as fundamental truths about the human condition and how people develop and thrive. The following are taken from one chapter within one of Rogers' books. The book is 'On Becoming a Person', the chapter is 'This is Me'. All the messages are directly quoted from Rogers' work, the categorisation of them is mine.

> *"We learn more by looking for the answer to a question and not finding it than we do from learning the answer itself"*
>
> Lloyd Alexander

Authenticity
- o In my relationships with other persons I have found that it does not help, in the long run, to act as though I were something that I am not;
- o I find I am more effective when I can listen acceptantly to myself, and can be myself.

Communicating with others
- o I have found it of enormous value when I can permit myself to understand another person;

# My Discoveries

- I have found it enriching to open channels whereby others can communicate their feelings, their perceptual worlds, to me;
- Evaluation by others is not a guide for me.

Acceptance
- I have found it highly rewarding when I can accept another person;
- The more I am open to the realities in me and in the other person, the less I find myself wishing to rush in to 'fix things'.

Experience
- Experience is, for me, the highest authority;
- I enjoy the discovering of order in experience;
- The facts are friendly (every bit of evidence one can acquire, in any area, leads one that much closer to what is true);
- What is most personal is most general
- Life, at its best, is a flowing, changing process in which nothing is fixed.

Positivity
- It is my experience that persons have a basically positive direction.

There are many insights here into the human condition and how we develop, the above extracts only touch the surface of Rogers' writings and thoughts. Although Rogers was not attempting to relate any of these observations to organisations, for me they are critical in helping us to understand some of the dynamics that can affect an organisation at a micro level.

> *"For wayfarers of all times, the right strategy for skillfully spreading the Way essentially lies in adapting to communicate. Those who do not know how to adapt stick to the letter and cling to doctrines, get stuck in forms and mired in sentiments – none of them succeed in strategic adaptation"*
>
> *Zhantang*

To take a few examples, let's look at authenticity. For the past three years I have been attending a five day developmental 'summer school' in Wales. This is run by an organisation called PSMW (Public Service Management Wales). It is attended by over 200 senior managers from across Wales who have the opportunity to listen to some of the best speakers from across the world. It is also a wonderful opportunity to have quality time to reflect on practice.

The topics of conversation centre on managerial excellence. Across all three of these summer schools I have identified patterns; common features that just keep popping up. And most prominent of these is authenticity – genuineness – an ability to be who you are. This is something Rogers talks about a lot, a trait that is about being who you are, identifying with your essence rather than your multiple personas.

Part of that quality of authenticity is an ability, an openness, a willingness to allow others to be authentic too. At a simple level, to encourage open and honest communication. I have a strongly held belief that if individuals within organisations were able to be more open and honest with each other, in a positive and 'healthy' way, those organisations would be more efficient and productive. Fewer problems would occur and when they did occur (as they always will) they would be resolved at an early stage.

Other aspects of Rogers' work refer to the power and order of experience (see next section), listening, and the positive nature of individuals. All these support a view that people thrive and grow when given the right environment and conditions. But how do we provide this – what is it we actually need to DO to assist this process?

> *"Look within. Within is the fountain of good, and it will ever bubble up, if thou wilt ever dig"*
>
> Marcus Aurelius

And so onto my next discovery, a very personal one that did not consciously emanate from any writings of others. And if it is true, it has a significant impact on how we attempt to develop and train our workforce (and ourselves).

## Discovery 3 – Life is like a jigsaw

Why is it that some people 'get it' and some people don't? Why is it that some people respond to training (apparently) and some people don't? Why is it that some people are awarded a University Degree and have virtually no common sense?

This is perhaps the most challenging and controversial proposition I am going to share with you, because if it is true, it has a profound impact on how we do 'business'.

Let me pick up on two things Carl Rogers said – 'experience is, for me, the highest authority' and 'I enjoy the discovering of order in experience'. The first statement is probably not something you would have trouble buying into. In my view it's the main reason so many people come out of higher education unable to deal with and respond to simple situations. They have absorbed (remembered) a wide range of theoretical information, and, to give the system some credit, made links and drawn conclusions that demonstrate more in-depth understandings and connections; but they haven't lived it! And, as Rogers proposes – experience is the HIGHEST AUTHORITY.

> *"Not I – Not anyone else, can travel that road for you, You must travel it for yourself"*
>
> *Walt Whitman*

Because we have come to understand this we have developed learning opportunities that link theory with practice; on the job training that complements academic programmes. They come in many forms and changing titles, including Apprenticeships. Do they work? In many cases yes, but in my experience even this integration of theory with practice still does not really impact on a significant minority of learners. Why is this?

Let's look at that other observation of Rogers – 'I enjoy the discovering of order in experience'. This is an observation that relates to retrospective analysis – i.e. if we look back on our lives we can often see patterns and 'moments' of clarity. Patterns that indicate that there is some form of order to our development. Moments that indicate that there is a timeliness to understanding.

If you have children, or you work with or know children, or even if you were a child yourself at some time (!), you might have observed something. An adult can attempt to give a child some advice (a sort of training) and it goes totally over their head. More than that, they may actively resist it. Then in 10 years time they turn round to you as a parent, teacher, youth worker, significant adult and say 'you know when you told me X, well I now suddenly realise what you meant' – Eureka!

What will have prompted that moment of learning is an experience that meant something to that individual. Where there was a connection between thinking and knowing. But why did it mean something at that moment in time? The answer was always there wasn't it? In fact in the example above, the answer was given by a significant other 10 years ago. What was missing was the connection, that realisation that made it true for that individual, as against a proposition verbalised by another.

This leads me into what I have called the Jigsaw of Life. My analogy is that life is a jigsaw. When we are born we are given a few pieces. These pieces are mostly rooted in 'instinct', those things that enable us to survive in the first few days of life. How to breathe, how to ask for food etc.

As we grow older all the answers (other pieces of the jigsaw) are out there. They are literally around us all the time. They are there when we observe the world around us, when we read books, in what people tell us. In everything we see, hear, feel and do.

However, in order to 'see' them we need to either search them out or recognise them when they present themselves. They may present themselves in a number of ways; through accidental or incidental contact, or through deliberate interventions (e.g. other people trying to tell us something).

> *"Again, you can't connect the dots looking forward; you can only connect them looking backwards. So you have to trust that the dots will somehow connect in your future. You have to trust in something - your gut, destiny, life, karma, whatever. This approach has never let me down, and it has made all the difference in my life"*
>
> Steve Jobs

Now here is the critical point. Think about how a jigsaw works. Actually, think about how a jigsaw would work if we were just given the first few pieces of one corner and not given the cover of the box – i.e. we had no indication of what the final picture looked like. What would that mean?

Well for a start, think how hard it would be to recognise and understand the significance of pieces of the jigsaw that did not fit with our emerging world view. Don't forget, all the pieces are laid out there in front of us, scattered around in front of us each and every day of our lives. In some cases people might even be saying – 'Hey, I've done this jigsaw before, you see this bit here, this is where it goes'. Some other people may even say to you 'I've completed my jigsaw and I know yours is the same as mine, let me complete it for you'!

This latter group are what I call life's missionaries, people who have (they think) discovered some larger meaning and want to, almost literally, convert you. This larger meaning could range from some level of profound spiritual understanding, through to how to become the world's most effective business leader!

Now let me ask you a simple question. If you have ever tried completing a jigsaw, how annoying is it when somebody tells you where the next piece fits? More importantly (for those who just like to 'win' and get things finished, however its done), how helpful is it when somebody gives you the next piece of the jigsaw in terms of you completing the whole picture for yourself? Does this actually help you to become competent at jigsaws? I would suggest it doesn't. It doesn't because you have not made the connections yourself, you have not linked one piece of the picture to the other, you have not analysed the edges in order to see if there is a natural fit between the pieces.

As a slight divergence let me briefly tell you about the time after my father died. It hurt. I cried (something I did not do very often). It made me re-evaluate my life in terms of meaning and what I was going to do with my life. I started to search for something. I didn't know what; all I knew was that there must be something out there beyond what I was currently experiencing. That desire to look beyond the obvious and superficial was not a new thing, but it was greatly fuelled by this significant event in my life.

As a result I visited a lot of spiritually related groups in order to see what they had to say, what they believed, what guided them. This included more traditional religions, through to what might be considered unconventional sects. What struck me was how sincerely and passionately each group, and each person in that group, believed in their version of the truth. What also struck me was that most were very sure their way was THE way and if I bought into that I would be 'saved'.

This led me to an obvious conclusion. All these groups can't be right. And if they all can't be right most of them must be wrong! So how do I find out who has really got the answer.

This led me to a chance encounter with a Swedish man dressed in orange. At the time I was making and selling my own hand-made pottery in Chester market. This intriguing guy came up to me and we had a conversation which led me to reading a book by a man called Bhagwan Shree Rajneesh. The book was called 'Neither This Nor That – Reflections on a Zen Master'. Ultimately, this also led to me travelling to Poona, India, to meet Mr Rajneesh.

Now, this is clearly a whole story in itself, but let me stress one important point. I was not only drawn to this man because of the eloquence of what he said, but the simple fact that he said everyone has to find their own way – their own understanding. There are many paths to the top of the mountain. Now this I could relate to. This was as near to the truth as I had found. And importantly, I was READY to hear what he had to say to me. If somebody had introduced me to him five years before, his teachings may have gone totally over my head – making no connections with my current jigsaw.

So back to the here and now (a very important place). What relevance does this talk of jigsaws and journeys have to this book in relation to organisations and organisational development?

Quite simply I am proposing to you that in order to move people from where they are you need to tap into their current world view. It is no good attempting to engage people by sharing your own world view. That will have little resonance or meaning for them unless you are lucky. You need to allow them to identify whatever issues you are attempting to address based on their own direct experiences, their current world view, their emerging jigsaw of the world. And as you will see later, this is exactly what Appreciative Inquiry does.

## Discovery 4 – Contact and stickiness

I am going to talk a little bit about Aikido, one of the Martial Arts that has its origins in Japan and the East. I had practiced Aikido for nearly 30 years before having to stop due to a developing knee weakness. There are many books that have translated martial arts into management practice and I have read none of them. However, I am going to share with you some key discoveries, based on my own direct experience, that link to the themes in this book.

Aikido appealed to me because of its focus on defence and its maintenance of tradition. I had practiced Jujitsu and Karate prior to this time, but it appeared to me that Aikido had generally maintained the high levels of personal discipline and etiquette that many other martial arts had lost to some degree. I was also fortunate enough to discover one of the best teachers (Sensei) in the world, right on my doorstep. His name was Terry Ezra and he had totally committed himself to Aikido to the extent that he purchased an old church in Birkenhead near Liverpool, and dedicated his life to sharing his skills and knowledge.

> *"As soon as you concern yourself with the 'good' and 'bad' of your fellows, you create an opening in your heart for maliciousness to enter. Testing, competing with, and criticizing others weaken and defeat you"*
>
> *Morihei Ueshiba – founder of Aikido*

So what is unique about Aikido? Maybe nothing. Much of the teaching is very similar to other martial arts in relation to using and focusing Ki, also referred to as Qi or Chi. In traditional Chinese culture, Qi is an active principle forming part of any living thing and is frequently translated as life energy, life force, or energy flow. The breakdown of the word Aikido is Ai (joining, unifying, harmonising) – Ki (spirit, energy) – Do (way, path).

One of the relatively unique aspects of Aikido, however, is the emphasis on 'contact', or as Terry often used to refer to it – stickiness. This links to the joining or harmonising aspect. When you are attacked, rather than blocking or moving away from the attack, you usually step slightly to the side and deflect the strike. If you are a martial artist you might be saying – 'lots of martial arts do this' – i.e. deflect the attack. However, in Aikido we add the 'stickiness' factor!

> *"Opponents confront us continually, but actually there is no opponent there. Enter deeply into an attack and neutralize it as you draw that misdirected force into your own sphere"*
>
> *Morihei Ueshiba – founder of Aikido*

This stickiness factor involves having 'contact' with your attacker (Tori) – i.e. almost literally sticking to him/her with the part of your body that has made contact with the attack – usually the hand or arm. The defender (Uke) then starts to harmonise with the attacker whilst initiating an Aikido technique, maintaining the initial contact with partner. This requires a high degree of sensitivity and control. These Aikido techniques are often referred to as 'joining' (Ai) with partner, often to the point where there is little distinction between Tori and Uke. In fact, very often there is an interchange between Tori and Uke as the contact is maintained – i.e. if both are Aikido trained and maintaining contact with partner, the distinction between who is attacking and who is defending can be a dynamic and changing process.

Another aspect of Aikido that sticks (sorry) with me is that of being present in the moment. There is currently growing interest in the business world in mindfulness, this centres on being in the 'here and now'. There is also reference to 'turning towards' the unpleasant and seeking out the pleasant. This is on the basis that there is increasing evidence that mindfulness can help people to have an improved ability to communicate well, improved creativity and a general ability to respond to difficult situations more efficiently.

> *"Be grateful even for hardship, setbacks, and bad people. Dealing with such obstacles is an essential part of training in Aikido"*
>
> *Morihei Ueshiba – founder of Aikido*

Within Aikido (and other martial arts) it is not really a choice, assuming you want to finish the night in some sort of good physical shape! If you are practicing attack and defence with another person, and there is any sort of genuineness about this, your mind strays at your peril. So Aikido literally demands you being in the here and now. And the more you are in touch with yourself and your environment the more effective you are in dealing with your attacker, in short, your survival chances rise.

So, what has any of this got to do with organisational development, Appreciative Inquiry, or anything else vaguely related to the themes in this book?

Let's go back to typical organisational behaviour, typical human behaviour. People naturally like to identify problems, usually problems that are associated with other groups or individuals. They also like to fix things, it is a natural tendency. It appeals to our egos and it appeals to our sense of wanting to make a difference (the potentially positive aspect). Of course, egos are highly apparent in physical combat, the desire to triumph over the other – to win.

We often refer to fight or flight within any scenario that involves challenge. We either face the situation and fight it, or we run away - flight. Again, this could relate to challenges at work that require response or action, or to actual physical challenge or attack.

> *"Is it hard?*
> *Not if you have the right attitudes. Its having the right attitudes that's hard."*
>
> Robert M. Pirsig

Aikido offers a third way, neither fight nor flight. Aikido trains the aikido practitioner (aikidōka) to neither attack nor run away, rather to become one with the attacker, to embrace, join, harmonise with the attacker through movement and contact.

It is the same with Appreciative Inquiry. We do not start from a position of attack – i.e. what is the problem, who is to blame etc. Nor do we seek to run away from the problems (a common misconception people have of Appreciative Inquiry). What we do is to embrace the problem, recognise it and reframe it in a way that avoids conflict but ultimately results in victory - actions that address real business issues!

I also touched on the subject of mindfulness. Interestingly this is not something that Appreciative Inquiry actively promotes or explicitly includes. However, I would argue that because the process of Appreciative Inquiry is totally engaging, this produces naturally high levels of mindfulness – i.e. participants focus intently on the task, as with martial arts. I am sure this is an area that could be explored more within Appreciative Inquiry and that this naturally occurring phenomena could be exploited in a more explicit way.

## Discovery 5 – Life is a journey

Let's finish the discoveries right back where I started, the inspiration for the title of my book – Zen and the Art of Motorcycle Maintenance by Robert M Pirsig. I could have called the book lots of things but somehow the notion of the journey has always captivated me. I nearly always use it when talking to groups, explaining that everything is a journey. We are all on individual journeys and organisations are on organisational journeys. And these journeys are all quite simply about travelling from A to B. Where are we now (A), where do we want to get to (B), and how are we going to get there (the journey).

Organisations all do this, formally and informally, but often they forget the most important part, how to take people with you. And the bigger the organisation the harder this becomes.

But first of all I want to tell you about the event that finally prompted me to write this book. It had been 'brewing' for many years, but this event was the catalyst. Why it was the catalyst I do not know, I haven't analysed it, but the commitment was made there and then.

> "We take a handful of sand from the endless landscape of awareness around us and call that handful of sand the world"
>
> Robert M. Pirsig

Earlier this year I attended a training course entitled 'Human Interactions Laboratory' in Italy. It was part of my own continuing professional development in relation to Appreciative Inquiry. I had attended a number of residential training courses on Appreciative Inquiry but wanted something that took my learning onto another level. The course appeared (and was) very intriguing because it applied Appreciative Inquiry thinking and practice to human interactions at a very fundamental level. It involved a small group of people in a 'T Group' experience.

Wikipedia describes a T Group as an experience 'where participants themselves (typically, between eight and 15 people) learn about themselves (and about small group processes in general) through their interaction with each other. They use feedback, problem solving, and role play to gain insights into themselves, others, and groups'.

> "Life is either a daring adventure or it is nothing"
>
> Helen Keller

We did not use role play and the exercise was 'framed' by Appreciative

Inquiry – in other words we carried out a number of Appreciative Inquiry exercises (Discovery and Dream) before the T group experience. This was important because T Groups (sometimes called Encounter Groups) can be destructive if managed badly (and some are), but the framing of the T Group with Appreciative Inquiry significantly minimises this possibility.

It is very hard for me to describe to you what a T Group is. In our case it was essentially a small group of people from all over the world (England, Scotland, Switzerland, Australia, South Africa) sitting together in a circle for four full days with some guidelines on the wall. There was no 'agenda' or any other form of guidance in relation to what we should talk about or do (apart from the guidelines). The guidelines encouraged us to do things like staying in the here and now (aka mindfulness), give feedback not advice and to be aware of assumptions.

> "...to arrive in the Rocky Mountains by plane would be to see them in one kind of context, as pretty scenery. But to arrive after days of hard travel across the prairies would be to see them in another way, as a goal, a promised land"
>
> Robert M. Pirsig

I have a friend who would describe this as very 'hippy'. Some of you will probably be having a similar reaction to what is undoubtedly an unconventional approach to personal development. All I can tell you is that I ultimately found it quite a profound experience, and it was certainly part of my journey in terms of understanding myself and others. At my time in life I feel it is often quite hard to find experiences that are substantially different than previous experiences, but this ticked that box fully. Again, I was willing to put myself 'out there' and see what happened, in my view an extremely important aspect of growth and development, in being able to find the next pieces of my personal jigsaw.

I initially decided I was going to take a plane to Italy, but then thought 'hell no', why not travel down on my motorbike, my 18-year old BMW R1100R. I have had motorbikes nearly all my adult life, but never been on a 'proper' trip – here was the opportunity. It was going to be uncomfortable (there is no such thing as a comfortable motorcycle seat after 3 hours), expensive and dangerous (motorbike + foreign roads and laws = danger), but that was part of the attraction.

This trip was prompted by many things including photographs of my father sitting on his BSA motorbike and his trip to Switzerland before I was born. Also the book I had first read when I was in my 20s called 'Zen and the Art of Motorcycle Maintenance'. And finally my wish to extend my own understanding of this thing called Appreciative Inquiry. In particular, I wanted a new type of experience that would help me to feel more alive again!

The whole trip would be a book in itself. It ended in me having a collision with another motorbike in Lyon, France – but, to state the obvious, I survived. There was the danger box ticked! But the important thing was I went on to write this book.

But I would like to return to Zen and the Art of Motorcycle Maintenance. The book describes a 17 day road trip by the author, Robert M. Pirsig, and his son. The book sold over 5 million copies worldwide and was initially rejected by 121 publishers, more than any other bestselling book according to the Guinness Book of Records. There are many themes in the book, including the Author's discovery of himself after a period of mental illness and memory loss.

> "Only those who speak of what they have experienced have confidence"
>
> Hermann Hess

Another key theme is the Author's search for the true meaning of 'good' or 'quality'. Pirsig proposes that to truly experience quality one must both embrace and apply it within each moment or situation. He describes the approach of his friend John, who chooses not to learn how to maintain his expensive new motorcycle. John simply hopes for the best with his bike, and when problems do occur he often becomes frustrated and is forced to rely on professional mechanics to repair it. In contrast, Pirsig has an older motorcycle which he is usually able to diagnose and repair himself through the use of rational problem solving skills.

Within this story Pirsig talks about the tension between the 'romantic' approach to life and the 'classical' approach. The former is likened to his friend John who hopes for the best and chooses not to learn how to maintain his expensive new motorcycle. The latter is like Pirsig, who chooses to apply logic and repair the bike himself. At the beginning the reader is led to believe that the classical view is the important one, the view that analyses and values how things function. However, later in the book it becomes clear that he sees the romantic view of equal importance, in fact it is the relationship and interplay between the two that gives both value.

The broader message within the book for me is that of the motorcycle journey itself. Being on a machine that some would suggest is not the most comfortable, cost effective, or sensible way to travel. However, it connects the rider to the environment in a way that no plane or even car could do. It immerses them in the experience, in a journey that results in much higher levels of engagement and stimulation. Through this greater level of awareness new things are seen that might have been missed otherwise.

There are also deeper messages about the very nature of life and the human condition.

And how does all this link with Appreciative Inquiry. There are numerous issues that resonate including the need to slow down. To take time to look at things properly in order to reach a diagnosis. How people have their very own world view and how this can be very limited in terms of the wealth of knowledge and information 'out there'. How we dissect and compartmentalise things and often miss the whole. The importance of thinking laterally and flexibly. To be open to new possibilities.

All the above have relevance in relation to Appreciative Inquiry which is essentially an opportunity for self reflection. Critically, it is crafted in such a way as to allow people to think in new and creative ways about themselves, about the organisation they work for, or both.

## My discoveries - summing up

The discoveries I have shared with you have been drawn from fifty- plus years of direct experience. For that reason they are powerful and meaningful to me. However, do they have any validity in terms of scientific research? Would they stand up to a randomised controlled trial? How would they fare when set up for peer review?

The interesting thing with some of the robust scientific research over the years is that even this gets challenged. Ultimately, some of it gets disproven by new findings, bringing in additional evidence and learning. The fact is, it is extremely difficult to prove a theory or hypothesis beyond doubt; maybe even impossible. The variables are so complex and diverse that any theory is only as good as the evidence available at that time.

Modern science refers to something called 'empirical evidence'. Wikipedia defines this as being dependent on evidence or consequences that are observable by the senses. One of the other key factors for scientists is that these same obervations must be witnessed by others on a repeated basis. So, does this book contain empirical evidence? Admittedly, all my observations by their very nature are subjective, i.e. they have been directly observed by one person (yours truly). However, my proposition to you is that they are supported by the experiences of many other people 'out there', particularly those who use Appreciative Inquiry. Of course the main criticism of this could be that those people living in 'AI land' (including myself) are bound to support a theory that they are propounding, and that is often intrinsically linked to their work (and hence income). However, what I am trying to demonstrate in this book is that the Appreciative Inquiry approach makes total logical sense, by any measure, and that this is based on the experiences of a growing number of people. But here is the real test - is it supported by your experiences too?

> *"Creativity is just connecting things. When you ask creative people how they did something, they feel a little guilty because they didn't really do it, they just saw something. It seemed obvious to them after a while. That's because they were able to connect experiences they've had and synthesize new things"*
>
> Steve Jobs

So let me summarise my learning, weave together all the previous observations about the human condition, and see how much it concurs with your own direct experience, your world view, your emerging jigsaw...

**People basically have a positive direction.** This is an important foundational belief in relation to Carl Rogers' work and as you will see later links with the first assumption of Appreciative Inquiry in relation to organisations and groups;

**A focus on fixing problems often results in a blame culture which can be 'corrosive' within organisations and does not lead to sustainable change and improvement.** This is particularly true within low performing teams and organisations;

**Our, and others', view of what is right or wrong, good or bad, important or not important, is highly subjective.** What is most important and meaningful to us are our own experiences, as we have experienced them;

**In our communications with others it helps, in the long run, to be ourselves and to be authentic.** This is a powerful and repeated message from Rogers' work and is articulated by many thought leaders in relation to effective leadership. This is often supported by the ability and willingness to be open and to embrace new ideas in a creative way;

**When we create situations where others are able to communicate their true feelings and views, this is an enriching process that has value.** This explicitly stresses the importance of allowing and supporting others to be authentic and share their views and feelings about themselves and their work;

**Evaluation by others is not the most important guide and motivator in terms of helping us to decide how we should live our lives.** This again stresses the importance of personal experience and how this needs to be harnessed if change and improvement programmes are to have any chance of real success. As Rogers says, personal experience is the highest 'authority' in terms of helping us to understand and make sense of what is happening around us and how we should develop and move on;

**We need to be open to the things that are happening to us and around us all the time, minute by minute.** The more we are exposed to, and open to, these experiences (jigsaw pieces), the more chances we have to develop and move on. This process of being open to things that are occurring around us is aided by a mindful state of mind – being in the here and now. This is stressed by Pirsig and by the recent interest in mindfulness within the business sector. The reference to 'turning towards' the unpleasant and seeking out the pleasant also has a high level of resonance with the thinking behind Appreciative Inquiry as you will see at later parts within this book;

**There is an order to experience and understanding that indicates that learning has a timeliness about it** – i.e. we understand and learn when the time is right for us and when we have found other bits of our jigsaw that help make that new experience or learning make sense;

**When we think we are the only ones experiencing a particular emotion, or thinking in a particular way, we often discover that others are thinking and feeling those things also.** We will see later that Appreciative Inquiry facilitates this process of sharing key learnings and identifying the patterns across all people's experiences;

**Life (including organisational life) is a flowing, changing process where nothing is fixed.** To be sensitive to that flow and be able to respond in harmony with it, rather than attempting to fight it or run away from it, is a more effective strategy.

I am going to finish this section by answering some rhetorical questions. Do I think it is easy to be authentic all the time? Do I think it is easy to be highly aware and open to possibilities on a day to day basis? And maybe most importantly in relation to the subject of this book, Appreciative Inquiry, do I think it is easy to see all things through a 'glass half-full' lens – focusing on the positive rather than the negative?

> *"If the world is in constant flux, then cumulative learning is negated and the concept of knowledge rendered problematic. What is learned or 'known' at any given instant may be irrelevant to the next"*
>
> *Kenneth J Gergen*

Simple answer for me – No. I was initially someone who was drawn to focusing on what isn't working, what is wrong, so that I could then apply my analytical mind to solving the problems. However, for me, this is what made Appreciative Inquiry all the more important and powerful – i.e. when my mindset changed and I started to identify with the thinking behind it (Social Constructionism). In addition, Appreciative Inquiry provided a practical and logical framework to apply that thinking, the 5D cycle; it wasn't just about words and theory, it was also about practical application. And when looking at things in this way becomes more and more habitual, this starts to affect the way we think and who we are – i.e. how we 'operate' on a day to day level. Most importantly, this new way of thinking and framing problems actually produces improved and sustainable results.

And so with the people within your organisations. Appreciative Inquiry really can be used as a methodology to start changing the way people think about problems and organisational development and improvement – with tangible results at the end. So let's explore the first stage, the thinking bit, a little further.

*All kinds of examples from motorcycle maintenance could be given, but the most striking example of value rigidity I can think of is the old South Indian Monkey Trap, which depends on value rigidity for its effectiveness. The trap consists of a hollowed out coconut chained to a stake. The coconut has some rice inside which can be grabbed through a small hole. The hole is big enough so that the monkey's hand can go in, but too small for his fist with rice in to come out. The monkey reaches in and is suddenly trapped - by nothing more than his value rigidity. He can't revalue the rice. He cannot see that freedom without the rice is more valuable than capture with it.*

Robert M Pirsig – Zen and the Art of Motorcycle Maintenance

# 3. APPRECIATIVE INQUIRY - THE THEORY

### How I found Appreciative Inquiry

I discovered Appreciative Inquiry by chance. I was catching up with an ex work colleague on the telephone and she mentioned she had been on a one day Appreciative Inquiry workshop, run by the Local Authority she worked for. She was very enthusiastic about the day and her brief description, together with a fascination with the name (Appreciative Inquiry), was enough to send me on a steep learning curve.

At the time I was approximately three years into developing my own business. This built on what I knew best, or at least what I thought I knew best – organisational improvement and development. My foundation for this was my time working in both the education and care sectors followed by posts within government inspection for both areas. This was in addition to a range of other posts within the voluntary and private sectors.

> *"We are what we think. All that we are arises with our thoughts. With our thoughts we make the world"*
>
> Buddha

As an inspector I would go into an organisation (e.g. care provider, further education college, youth service etc.) and make judgements about how effective that service was. This would either be alone or as part of a large inspection team. Put simply, these judgements were based on what worked and what didn't work; strengths and weaknesses. The inspection team would then leave the organisation with a set of recommendations in order to 'fix' the weaknesses.

My experience of these inspections was mixed. They were very structured, with inspection frameworks that were either based on nationally agreed standards (care) or quality indicators (education). Within education there was a high degree of reliance on the judgements of a team of inspectors who came together for a 'moderation' process in order to agree grades against the inspection framework. These judgements were based on 'good features' and 'shortcoming' – or alternative language that was developed over time. However, the focus was firmly on the areas of weakness on the basis that it was these that were the drivers for the action plan.

Subsequently I worked with these same organisations in an independent capacity, usually post inspection. To do what? Yup, you guessed it – to respond to the recommendations, fix the things that were deemed weak. Now, at one level there is nothing wrong with this, but there was one glaring omission – a whole aspect of the organisation that was given little focus in terms of analysis. And that aspect was fundamentally – what was working in the organisation and why; and how could this be used as a catalyst for improvement.

> *"Man is not the creature of circumstances.*
> *Circumstances are the creatures of men"*
>
> Benjamin Disraeli

My experience of these inspections was mixed. To some degree I actually enjoyed the highly structured process, it appealed to the anal side of me and made logical sense. To some degree, however, I also fought against the level of 'tightness', the very strict boundaries (particularly within education) that did not allow for intuitive and creative thinking. Maybe this had something to do with the fact that I had originally trained and qualified as an Art teacher; now there's a lost cause!

In relation to specific inspections, I enjoyed some and did not enjoy others. And there was a pattern here. Perhaps unsurprisingly I tended to enjoy the inspections that went well and did not enjoy the inspections that graded the provider poorly. What I was witnessing (in retrospect) was a process that was generally supportive and confirming for those who were already doing a good job and, to a degree, damaging to those that didn't.

It seems really obvious doesn't it? Where organisations were deemed to have excellent practice this produced a self-sustaining feel good factor. We are doing these things really well, let's do more of them. The workforce felt good about themselves and the whole language within the organisation was generative.

Where organisations were deemed to be doing badly (and in particular where performance was deemed very poor), people felt negatively about themselves and inevitably blame followed. The managers blamed the staff, the staff blamed the managers, and everybody blamed the IT department! Responses were made to recommendations and very often on a superficial level identified problems were fixed; but actually the fabric and essence of the organisation remained 'broken' in my view.

OK – so at this point you might be thinking – 'yeah, but we don't work in an education or care establishment, nor do we get inspected'. What I suggest to you, however, is that this focus on problems is what most organisations do to some degree and in some way, formally or informally, structured or unstructured. This might be through structured management away days and business planning processes at a top level. It might be through appraisal and supervision processes at an individual level. Even if this is not part of formal and structured processes, isn't this way of thinking typical of the informal conversations that go on within organisations – what isn't working and who is to blame?

So let's go right back to my phone conversation and introduction to Appreciative Inquiry. Remember I was living in 'deficit world'. I was that man who went into organisations, told them what the problems were, then gave them recommendations on how to fix them. So what was it that turned my world upside down in terms of my assumptions about organisational change and improvement. What was it that challenged the clear logic that if you identify what the problems are and fix them you will ultimately ensure improvement?

Of course the answer to that question is the substance of this book and will be laid out as you read on. Essentially, however, what occurred was that a framework, a way of thinking and an accompanying structured methodology for delivery, was presented to me that made total sense. It made logical sense, and it made sense of other 'moments' and learnings throughout my life in relation to how we develop as individuals and organisations.

## Appreciative Inquiry Principles

The theories that support Appreciative Inquiry talk about how individuals and groups operate. Within 'AI world' they are generally expressed in one of two ways. The first are based on what are commonly referred to as the five principles of Appreciative Inquiry, the second are expressed as eight assumptions and are laid out in a slightly more simple and accessible manner.

## Social Constructionist theory

This has been mentioned earlier in the book and is the central theory underpinning Appreciative Inquiry. Social Constructionism proposes we develop meaning in our lives out of our experiences and in conversation with others. It also proposes that the language we use to describe things actually contributes to and shapes how we perceive the world around us.

You will see how this builds on discovery one in the last chapter – a glass half full. If you remember, this explained how two people can go through exactly the same event, but experience this very differently. Based on these different perceptions, they will then use totally different language to describe this event. Two men stood behind prison bars, one saw mud, the other saw stars!

> *"We do not describe the world we see, we see the world we describe"*
>
> *Joseph Jaworski*

Once people start describing their experiences to other people we have a whole new dynamic to the 'facts'. We might have two very different stories about that same experience. Within organisations, some people may focus on the negative aspects of events, others focus on the positive aspects and how they overcame the challenges. This creates a very different reality for themselves and for the people they interact with.

> *"I believe the real difference between success and failure in a corporation can be very often traced to the question of how well the organization brings out the great energies and talents of its people"*
>
> *Thomas J. Watson, Jr*

These stories start to almost literally have a life of their own that cannot be predicted or controlled by the organisation. This is one of the ways in which cultures are born and sustained. And these stories rarely occur within controlled structured settings (e.g. formal meetings). They take place at the lunch table or over coffee breaks. If they are all about how bad the organisation is and how overworked people are, then these stories will tend to shape the reality within the workforce. This is then going to be the kind of place they will build – an unhappy place that will probably never reach its full potential. A self fulfilling prophesy!

But if the stories people tell are about how good it is to work within the organisation, and the language they use about each other is mostly positive – then they see a different reality. And this will in turn affect the kind of workplace that develops - a more positive and productive environment.

Of course neither extreme ever happens within any group – i.e. there is a mixture of both positive and negative language, but what does vary is the balance and context of these conversations.

Somebody who is well known in this field of work is Ken Gergen. Gergen has been particularly concerned with fostering a 'relational' view of the self - where the 'traditional emphasis on the individual mind is replaced by a concern with the relational processes from which rationality and morality emerge'. He is also known for his comment 'I am linked therefore I am' as an answer to Descartes view 'I think, therefore I am'.

You can see here how social constructionism builds on the cognitive behavioural viewpoint, adding the dynamic of social intercourse. You can also hopefully see how relevant this is to the life of organisations, where at any one time hundreds of conversations may be occurring. And to take one of the assumptions of Appreciative Inquiry – 'reality is created in the moment, and there are multiple realities'.

## Simultaneity Principle

The Simultaneity Principle asserts that the questions we ask and the stories we share already hold the seeds of change. Change doesn't simply happen at the end of a process – it starts from the first moment we step in to ask the question or to tell a story. In other words 'the questions we ask determine what we find'. Inquiry and change are not separate moments but often happen simultaneously – inquiry is change, is intervention. This is part of the thinking behind Action Research.

For example a company facing a large staff turnover and wanting to retain staff could ask 'what do you think is causing people to leave us' or they could ask 'what are the things about this company you value most and have encouraged you to stay with us'.

Imagine the conversations, topics and emotions that would be buzzing around that company as a result of each of those questions.

What kind of company do you think people would start to find?

In the first example they will probably start seeing a place that is full of problems that result in people leaving for pastures new. In the second they will start seeing a place that is far more attractive and gives people lots of good reasons to work there.

In each case the very first question is already influencing the lens through which people are looking at their work place. This in turn will influence the culture of the workplace and direction in which it develops. The seeds of change are embedded in the first questions we ask.

So what questions are you asking the people around you?

**Poetic Principle**

The Poetic Principle proposes that we are constantly rewriting and reinterpreting our view of reality. It acknowledges the value and power of story telling as a way of sharing and gathering information and that these stories are constantly being re-written.

An organisation's past, present or future is an endless source of learning and can be open to many interpretations. It is also open to many possibilities.

For example, imagine a college where most of the students struggle with reading and writing. One teacher's story might be that these young people are limited and that teaching them is a struggle. Another teacher may share a different view and talk about a passion for seeing students succeed and focusing on their strengths and resilience. Seeing his work as a positive challenge each day.

*"You can't depend on your judgement when your imagination is out of focus"*

*Mark Twain*

At each moment everyone in that school has a choice about which story they want to identify with. They then have a choice about what story they tell to others. And so the 'Chinese whispers' goes on. An uncontrollable buzz, with each moment sowing the seeds of change within the organisation. The question is, can this inevitable process be harnessed into something positive?

The Poetic Principle also suggests that any organisation will have a 'collective story' that is influenced by all the different stories and interpretations of the individuals within it.

Just as we can appreciate the richness of different interpretations of a poem or book, we can also appreciate the value of each person's interpretation of our organisational story.

Changing the collective story involves freeing our imaginations and the imaginations of those around us. And rewriting our stories gives us the opportunity to create positive change.

How open are you to rewriting the story you tell about your organisation?

## Anticipatory Principle

This builds on the view that perceptions and behaviours are not only founded on what we have experienced in the past, but also on what we anticipate, imagine, or dream might happen in the future.

Our minds are like cinema projectors, constantly projecting images of what might be; and those images have a significant impact on how we behave in the here and now. When we talk to others within a group or organisation about the future we start to form a collective vision, and that vision affects how we behave and perceive the group or organisation in the present.

> *"The task of organisational leadership is to create an alignment of strengths in ways that make a system's weaknesses irrelevant"*
>
> *Peter Drucker*

Within organisations, management can spend all the time they want 'visioning' and writing mission statements. These mission statements may be cascaded throughout the organisation by formal communication channels. But if these visions are not created, shared and owned by everyone; 'everyone' will create their own images of the future through their own natural communication channels – i.e. informal conversation.

A classic example of this is often quoted in Appreciative Inquiry. This relates to the visions Winston Churchill helped create during the second world war – he did not focus on the seeming impossibilities of the situation, but rather on the rightness of the cause and the strengths within the British people. This created a shared national vision that resulted in very real positive actions, people behaving in ways that they might not have done otherwise. Regardless of your view about the pros and cons of war, this is a powerful example of how words can impact on a group of people, in this case a nation. Of course, ironically, exactly the same could be said of Hitler, but in this case his vision was one of power, domination and death.

### Positive Principle

The Positive Principle asserts the view that the momentum for change requires large amounts of positive affect and that people are (innately) positive systems – i.e. they respond to positive thoughts, ideas, knowledge, feedback etc. This is similar to many other theories including those of Carl Rogers and his assertions about the importance of 'unconditional positive regard'.

On this basis, repeated inquiries into why things are not working are less likely to produce the required momentum for change as inquiries into what is working and why.

This does not mean to say that problems should not be addressed. The whole basis for organisational development is that of improvement, and this requires that the organisation does things differently and more effectively. Part of this improvement will require, at times, decisive and assertive action including the recognition (for example) that some people are in the wrong job. However, Appreciative Inquiry addresses problematic areas within a positive framework (that of a desired future) and goes on to involve all stakeholders in a response strategy that they have co-created.

Powerful examples exist of the results of positive thought and belief. These include the Placebo and Pygmalion effects.

**The Placebo Effect** is a commonly known theory within the medical world. It relates to cases where some patients given a placebo treatment (typically a sugar pill) have a perceived or actual improvement in a medical condition. In these cases, the patient's belief that the medication (that is an inert substance) is going to make them better, does actually make them feel better.

One can argue whether 'feeling better' equates to actually being better, but the point is that in these patient's 'world' they are better than they were before.

The relevance to Appreciative Inquiry is the power of language, expectation and anticipation. If the language is positive, and the future image is positive, this usually brings about a positive frame of mind and a 'gravitation' towards this outcome.

It should be noted that the Placebo effect has been demonstrated equally to negative suggestion – i.e. inert substances have the potential to cause negative effects via the "nocebo effect" (Latin nocebo = "I will harm"). In this effect, giving an inert substance has negative consequences. Some would say that an extreme example of this is within folk magic and sticking pins in dolls. In these cases there are reports of the subject of the practice actually falling ill and dying.

**The Pygmalion effect**, or Rosenthal effect, refers to the phenomenon in which the greater the expectation placed upon people (e.g. children, students, employees etc.) the better they perform. The effect is named after Pygmalion, a Cypriot sculptor in a narrative by Ovid in Greek mythology, Pygmalion created a statue and fell in love with it. He began to pray for the statue to turn into a human. His wishes materialised one day and the statue became real.

The Pygmalion effect is a type of self fulfilling prophesy – i.e. if people believe something to be true it will be true (and the converse). In a study by Robert Rosenthal and Lenore Jacobson they showed that if teachers were led to expect enhanced performance from some children, then the children did indeed show that enhancement.

In an organisational context, the proposition is that if managers have high expectations of staff, those staff will rise to the occasion to some degree.

## The 8 Assumptions of Appreciative Inquiry

In addition to the five principles, the theory of Appreciative Inquiry is often defined within the context of eight assumptions.

These assumptions (from 'The Thin Book of Appreciative Inquiry' by Sue Hammond), seek to define the underlying principles of Appreciative Inquiry in a different, and more simple way. They have now become embedded in the narratives about Appreciative Inquiry as a way to help people understand the thinking and beliefs behind the approach.

1. In every society, organisation or group, something works;

2. What we focus on becomes our reality;

3. Reality is created in the moment, and there are multiple realities;

4. The act of asking questions of an organisation, or group, influences them in some way;

5. People have more confidence to journey to the future (the unknown) when they carry forward parts of the past (the known);

6. If we carry forward parts of the past, they should be what is best about the past;

7. It is important to value difference;

8. The language we use creates our reality;

You will see here that these assumptions cover the same ground as the five principles, but sometimes the language is more accessible.

## The theory – a summary

I hope that the core messages from both my own experiences and the principles and assumptions of Appreciative Inquiry are starting to appear clear and coherent. Again, the key question is – to what degree do they align with your own world view – essentially – do you agree with them?

Interestingly, even if you don't agree with some of them, this, in some weird and wonderful way, supports the overarching premise – i.e. that to engage people you need to start from their own experiences! If all you do is bring in outside people with the latest theory on this or that, you may fail from the start. For me, that is one of the most essential components of the Appreciative Inquiry process, and more of that in the next section. So let's just take stock of some of the key messages here…

## Positive direction and language

Maybe the first and underpinning message for me is that essentially people have a positive direction and generally want to do their best. Of course, as with all the assertions in this book, there are exceptions, but there is still an underlying and innate positivity in all or most people. Rogers put this well when he said – 'I am aware that out of defensiveness and inner fear individuals can and do behave in ways which are incredibly cruel, horrible, destructive, immature, regressive, anti-social, and hurtful (*how's that for a list!*). Yet one of the most refreshing and invigorating parts of my experience is to work with such individuals and to discover the strongly positive directional tendencies which exist in them, as in all of us, at the deepest level'.

Linking to this and taking it to another level, within all groups and organisations, some things work. This is Hammond's first assumption, the thing that again underpins the thinking and practice of Appreciative Inquiry, and one that drives the Discovery Stage of the 5D process.

Finally there is a recognition within Appreciative Inquiry that positivity is essentially infectious. Not just at a superficial and temporary level, but in a way that becomes embedded in our being over time. This links to a number of the principles and assumptions of Appreciative Inquiry and proposes that the conversations we have with other people, the words we use, the aspirations and dreams we share, become our joint reality.

## The power and timeliness of experience

Rogers said 'experience is the highest authority' and it cannot be said more simply and clearly than this for me. What we directly experience has the most power and influence over what we become and how we behave. It has most meaning for us.

The second element of this is about timeliness, and my proposition about the 'jigsaw' nature of our personal development. As I said earlier, this is perhaps the most controversial element of this book, but something I have come to believe is true. I have not read it anywhere (although I am sure I am not the first to suggest it) but it totally aligns with my 50+ years of experience of life. This is often interpreted by people as a fatalistic aspect of life i.e. things happen at the right time because they were meant to. I do not believe this. I think that 'things' are happening all the time – around us everywhere. But (and this is the critical bit), we will not see the very answers we need unless we have our eyes and ears open and the time is right. And what makes the time right? Being at the right stage in our very own jigsaw puzzle makes it right. Having the pieces in place that connect to that piece floating in the air in front of us.

In relation to training and organisational development these two assumptions have a very real and significant potential impact. To state these again, they would indicate that, as Rogers puts it – 'The judgements of others, while they are to be listened to, and taken into account for what they are, can never be a guide to me'.

If this is the case for many other people (and I put my hand up here) then what does this say about our training and development activity?

The ideas, views, opinions of others – whether they be external 'experts' or internal management do not have the influence and impact we might like to think they have. Any group of people will include individuals with extremely diverse experiences. These people will also have very different levels of knowledge and understanding based on these experiences. Essentially they will be in very different 'places' in their lives.

> *"At Microsoft there are lots of brilliant ideas but the image is that they all come from the top - I'm afraid that's not quite right"*
>
> Bill Gates

Any good trainer or change management specialist will tell you – 'start where people are at', but how do you do that? What usually occurs in these developmental processes is that standardised packages of training or interventions are put into place. These will 'take' some people with you, but not others. In fact the people you take with you are often the ones you didn't need to do the intervention with in the first place!

## Whole system approach

The scenarios above are based on the premise that management do actually engage with key stakeholders in order to drive forward programmes of change and improvement. Of course we know that this is often not the approach taken. Very often management huddle together on away days to apply their significant knowledge and expertise (why else are we paid all this money) in order to agree and implement their next business plan. Plans come out of businesses (and particularly local government) like confetti, but does this activity actually make a difference?

When I am talking to groups about this subject I usually speak about that journey from A to B. Everything is actually about that. Whether it is about individual or organisational development, it is about a journey. We then talk about what we need to know and do to go on this journey. In one way or another most organisations talk about knowing where A is – where they are now. They talk about knowing where B might be – where they want to get to. They talk about agreeing a plan – a set of actions that will take them from A to B. Sometimes they talk about slightly more sophisticated and complex issues like making sure A and B haven't changed and altering their plans to compensate. They might even discuss the process of evaluating when they have reached B in terms of impact assessment. Processes like Results Based Accountability (RBA) might be used to ensure they focus on outcomes for the customer and constantly measure themselves against baselines in order to 'turn the curve' (RBA speak for ensuring we change our 'trajectory' in a positive direction).

> *"Whatever you can do or dream you can, begin it. Boldness has genius, power and magic in it"*
>
> Goethe

So that's what organisations usually talk about. So what is it they often don't talk about, and certainly in my opinion don't adequately address?

Answer - involving the whole system. Engaging key stakeholders such as the workforce, customers, partners to:

- o 'exploit' their significant knowledge, skills, views and ideas;
- o get their active engagement in the process from the very start;
- o ensure buy-in and ownership of any resultant action plans.

## Chaos and flow

Rogers said 'life is a flowing, changing process where nothing is fixed'. One of Hammond's assumptions is that 'reality is created in the moment, and there are multiple realities'. Aikido teaches us not to resist or move away, but to maintain contact and 'go with the flow'. You might think at this point 'should I really bother', the dynamics of informal conversations ebbing and flowing seemingly without control sounds like total chaos. How can I even attempt to harness this in any sort of proactive and positive way?

My experience, based on working in and inspecting a broad range of organisations, is that they all have the potential (and possibly the tendency) towards chaos. An organisation is like a field. If the field is left to its own devices there will be little perceived order. Weeds and trees will grow in a seemingly random fashion, although certain natural laws and balances will emerge. However, what organisations want is order and productivity. They need to be able to grow their products or services as efficiently as possible. This means that rules need to be put into place and labour is required. Weeds need to be replaced with seeds of a specific type. The soil needs to be kept fertile and ploughed. Competition (insects) need to be recognised and controlled. Water needs to be applied on a regular basis and finally crops need to be picked, packaged and sold.

In the traditional organisational world this chaotic tendency has usually resulted in highly structured management supported by trained staff and effective systems and procedures. A good command and control system. How else can we do it – right?

However, lurking in the background, within the dark corners and cracks of the organisation, there is always a natural tendency towards chaos. If the water can't be found, if the insects start adapting, if the staff go on strike – the natural order will soon return – anarchy, chaos!

However, there are a few farmers, supported by new ways of thinking, who try to work with the land. They recognise that a purely 'top down' approach is possibly not the most effective and efficient way to work. They certainly realise that fighting to combat nature is a costly battle, in more ways than one.

Widely recognised responses to this include the use of 'set aside'. This recognises that the land cannot maintain its fertility without having a natural break. This results in fields having a rotation of use. Other approaches involve using certain plants that have been found to deter specific insects in a natural way. All these approaches essentially involve 'listening' to the land.

So it is with our organisations. Many organisations still essentially use systems of command and control that focus the decision making at senior management level. Some of these include superficial levels of consultation, mainly involving 'this is what we have decided – what do you think of it'. The reality is that decisions are already made and the 'consultation' process actually makes little difference to the outcome.

These top down structures can and do work. However, like in our field analogy, there is a constant battle going on to resist the innate tendency towards chaos. And the larger the organisation the greater potential for chaos there is.

So how does this chaotic tendency present itself? It presents itself in the micro moments within organisations and within human interaction. All those totally uncontrolled, unstructured, unplanned, unrecorded, unanticipated communications that occur in every organisation every hour of every working day. In fact, with the rise of online social media, these conversations also occur increasingly outside of traditional work hours. So what is the choice? Work against it in order to control it, or work with it in order to harness it?

The truth within the slightly simplistic and polarised examples above is that management actually needs to use all the tools it has at its disposal, including command and control. However, the reality is that many do not even recognise some of the alternative tools at their disposal, never mind know how to use them!

At this point let me speak briefly of the work of Ralph Stacey. He is Professor of Management at the Business School of the University of Hertfordshire and a Member of the Institute of Group Analysis. He is also a founding member of, and currently supervisor on, an innovative Masters and Doctoral program in complexity and organisational change. He proposed that organisations can be operating on a number of levels ranging from traditional top-down management through to experiencing the 'edge of chaos'.

Stacey has spent many years exploring how the complexity sciences might provide a new way of understanding stability and change in organisations. His work on complex responsive processes presented a view that shifts the understanding of complexity from adaptive systems to responsive processes of human relating.

Stacey originally proposed a matrix based on two dimensions with regards to management of organisations: certainty and agreement. Certainty depends on the quality of the information base that supports decisions in organisations. Many organisations attempt to facilitate decision making by use of rational analysis, underpinned by a constantly changing (and fashionable) range of tools. These are generally introduced and initiated by experts or specialists in their field. In many cases these processes result in useful data that leads to more informed and successful strategies. However, Stacey suggested that these strategies are based on a range of assumptions and variables that introduce high levels of uncertainty. These centre on the impact of external, and usually relatively unpredictable and uncontrollable factors – people! The degree of agreement among the people (directly and indirectly) involved in any project in relation to what and how things should be done is a critical factor in determining success.

More recently Stacey argues that life is complex all the time and not just in those times that are 'far from certainty' and 'far from agreement'. This is because change is inextricably linked to the everyday conversations within organisations. This means that even in the most seemingly ordinary conversations something might happen that has more significant consequences. On this basis there are no 'levels of complexity'. Perhaps therefore every moment of life (including organisational 'life') holds the seeds of complexity and change (my comment not Stacey's).

But again the question arises – what do we actually DO in response to these challenges facing us? The multitude of conversations that are taking place in our organisations each and every hour of every day of every year. The rumbling lava below the surface that could explode at any time.

*We're living in topsy turvy times, and I think what causes the topsy turvy is inadequacy of old forms of thought to deal with new experiences. I've heard it said that the only real learning results from hangups, where instead of expanding the branches of what you already know, you have to stop and drift laterally for a while until you come across something that allows you to expand the roots of what you already know.*

*Robert M Pirsig – Zen and the Art of Motorcycle Maintenance*

# The application of AI – the 5D cycle

**Deliver**

**Design**

**Dream**

**Discover**

**Define**

## 4. THE APPLICATION OF AI - THE 5D CYCLE

This section is a practical guide to applying the 5D Cycle, a tried and tested methodology that takes participants through a series of stages. Stages of a process that build on each other in a sequential and supportive manner that results in real change and improvement. From here on in I am going to refer to Appreciative Inquiry as AI unless it is quoted by others.

These stages take people through a process of:-

- Defining what is going to be done and how
- Discovering the best of what is and why it is occurring
- Dreaming what could be – aspirations for the future
- Designing and planning
- Delivering the actions and addressing sustainability

Before I get into the detail of the process, let me try and define AI within a couple of sentences. If you start to develop an interest in AI you will attempt to do this yourself, usually because people will ask you the question – 'what is AI?'. You will ultimately come up with your own definition, but here is one of mine for starters. In this case it is within the context of organisational development (OD).

*'Appreciative Inquiry engages with key stakeholders to identify and build on what is working best within an organisation. The focus can be on whole organisational transformation or specific elements of operation. It supports participants to discover what is working and why, building on this to deliver an aspirational future. Because the process starts with participant's own experiences and everyone contributes to defining the future, people take ownership of actions and the process is sustainable into the long term'.*

The thinking behind AI can be applied in lots of ways, the 5D Cycle just happens to be the methodology that most people are familiar with. In general I 'package' AI in one of two ways. I either train people in AI so that they can use it with others, or I facilitate a developmental process using AI. Increasingly I also use a combination of both.

When the 5D Cycle is used for facilitating a developmental process there is actually no need to refer to it by name – i.e. either the 5D Cycle or AI. It is only necessary for the facilitator themselves to understand the thinking behind AI (the principles and assumptions) and how to apply the process (the 5D Cycle or other applications that build on the thinking).

One other point by way of context and background, the 5D Cycle used to be referred to (and still is by some) as a 4D Cycle. For me the 5D Cycle makes more sense. Not that it adds or takes away anything from the original, but because it emphasises the importance of Defining (first D) our themes – what we are going to focus on, and how. This was always present in the 4D process, but the extra D embeds it as one of the main stages, giving it the significance it deserves.

So let's look at the whole process and then interrogate all the tasks and elements within each stage.

The 5D Cycle is usually illustrated by a circle on the basis that it is part of an ongoing cycle that can, and generally should, be repeated and embedded within the processes of an organisation. The graphic above, however, uses stones to depict the importance of one stage building on another, to stress how each supports the other in a process of ultimate delivery and action.

I will emphasise this within other sections of the book but let me make it clear now – AI results in people doing things. These 'things' should make a tangible difference to the business or service and when this occurs it will result in greater levels of customer satisfaction with a product or service. This works because key stakeholders take ownership of actions and this is sustained into the long term.

So to the stages, starting with…

The application of AI – Define

## Stage 1 – Define

As anyone who has project managed an initiative will know, it is critically important to establish clear terms of reference, understand what your 'end game' is in terms of impact, and plan the logistics of delivery. Within the Define Stage these elements are addressed, but Define also focuses on another key issue, the use of language. Remember the 8 assumptions of AI and the assertion that the act of asking questions of an organisation, or group, or individual influences them in some way.

This is the first opportunity to decide what the focus (the topics) of the AI process is going to be and how questions are going to be crafted to provide an effective and inspirational catalyst for constructive dialogue.

> "Before everything else, getting ready is the secret of success"
>
> Henry Ford

Note - you may find that will need to return to this section on Define again, after you have read more about the other stages of the process. This will put the Define Stage into more context.

These are the key tasks within the Define Stage.

## Task 1 – Planning

The following are some of the elements that need to be discussed and agreed during the planning stage, some obvious, some less so:

- o What is the purpose mission statement of the organisation? How can this be used within the process in order to agree the topics? If the organisation has not got an explicit mission statement or statement of purpose can this be explored with participants within the process (usually at the beginning)?

> "Management by objective works - if you know the objectives. Ninety percent of the time you don't"
>
> Peter Drucker

- o What areas of development or issues (the topics) do management want to focus on and how have these arisen? What do they want more of? Are these uniquely management issues or are they generally recognised across the organisation?

- o Do management and other key decision makers see themselves being directly involved in the process? The involvement of senior managers and other key decision makers nearly always enhances the process and in particular ensures actions can be signed off as quickly as possible.

o Who are the stakeholders and where are they located? Make sure they are all identified and there is a full exploration of how they can be involved. As a general rule the wider the stakeholder group, the more successful the process. If the organisation has a number of locations how can they all be involved, either directly or as part of some type of cascade process?

> *"Most discussions of decision making assume that only senior executives make decisions or that only senior executives' decisions matter. This is a dangerous mistake"*
>
> *Peter Drucker*

o Who could contribute to a core planning and implementation team? Depending on the size of the implementation, some form of shared planning and implementation is useful and helps to start upskilling people. This should ideally be a group who show a natural interest in the process or who have been identified as people who are naturally 'glass half full' thinkers.

o Should the delivery of the whole process be attempted within an AI Summit – i.e. everybody coming together for a series of days in a workshop activity? The alternative is to conduct elements of the process in other ways. This can range from cascaded one-to-one meetings, small group activity, questionnaires etc. It is always the case that personal face-to-face communication is preferential to written communication. Having said that, any form of communication is better than none at all, even if this is only for sections of the identified group. The stages of AI that are mostly delivered in alternative ways (to a Summit) are the Discovery and Dream stages.

o What are the expected outcomes of the process at a managerial and wider level?

o Do you want to include any form of evaluation of impact? If so, baselines will need to be agreed, along with KPIs (key performance indicators). It should be noted that this is not a normal part of the process, but it is acknowledged that organisations using AI may want to establish effectiveness in order to inform wider application.

- o How is the process going to be introduced to the workforce and other stakeholders? How are they going to be involved in influencing the questions for the Discovery and Dream stages?

- o Where should workshops be held in order to ensure a conducive environment and sufficient space for pairs and groups to break out?

- o Will there be any type of launch of the AI Summit – i.e. an added benefit of the process could be some form of promotion or PR outcome?

All of the above will lead to an implementation plan. At the lower end of the scale this plan may only involve an external AI facilitator delivering a one-day programme for a small team of people. One day is the absolute minimum that the latter four stages of the 5D cycle will take within a workshop setting (note – this will be after initial planning through the Define Stage). This would usually be in a situation where the client is an SME (small or medium sized enterprise) within a single location. However, in the great majority of cases this will not be long enough to fully implement the process. Don't forget that even if the team is small, there will be other stakeholders to consider – e.g. customers, service users, partners, suppliers, advocates etc.

At the higher end of the scale, within a medium sized organisation, the process will take at least two to four days for the whole cycle. Even then other activity will take place after the 'main event', and possibly during it. The aim here is to engage as many people within the stakeholder group as possible, even if some of this does not involve participation in the main workshops.

Within very large organisations, with multiple locations and possibly thousands of staff and other stakeholders, the process requires significant planning and will take an extended period (at least six months). This does not mean that there will be six months of activity, but that this length of time will be required for full roll out and completion. Inevitably in an organisation this size, some people will usually need to be engaged in other ways other than attendance at the workshops (also described as Summits). Change takes time and requires a cascade effect beyond the initial interventions.

## Task 2 - Topic choice

One of the key elements of the planning stage above describes the focus of the AI exercise and the topic choices. Getting the topic choices right is pivotal to the success of the whole process. The essential rule here is that the topics need to be meaningful - they need to be based on some aspect of the business (or individual when used as a coaching or individual development tool) that is acknowledged as requiring movement or change. A compelling topic; something people want more of and can't wait to start moving towards!

> *"The most serious mistakes are not being made as a result of wrong answers. The truly dangerous thing is asking the wrong questions"*
>
> *Peter Drucker*

In business, topics need to be based on something that most people within the organisation would recognise as requiring action, the more pressing that requirement the better. Why is this the case? Well, from a very practical viewpoint there is little chance any organisation will dedicate the required resources (people, time) into an exercise that could take anything from days to months to deliver, unless it is addressing a pressing business issue. Secondly, for people to fully engage with the process they also need to be able to identify with the topics as something that requires change and improvement, something that will ultimately benefit them and their organisation.

Topics can be broad or narrow. They can be as broad as conducting an organisational wide self-evaluation exercise, or as narrow as the introduction of a new IT system (or aspect of it). Specific topics can focus on issues such as human interaction (e.g. management, communication, etc), environment (e.g. planning a new extension or office location), or systems and processes (e.g. appraisal, supervision, health and safety, equality and diversity etc). Actually, once the process has started, these areas will usually arise as contributory factors anyway – i.e. a system issue is rarely just down to systems and processes. In fact most system issues are linked to human elements such as communication and relationships.

This is one of the strengths of the AI approach, it takes a much more lateral view of any issue, avoiding the assumption that a presenting problem is the only area that needs to be dealt with.

## Task 3 - Forming questions

Once topics are agreed, questions have to be written in a way that acts as an effective catalyst to the whole process. There are some guidelines for writing effective questions that will be used within both the Discovery and Dream stages. Let's take these one by one.

1. **Context** - The context of the questions is fundamental. As stated above, they need to focus on issues that are meaningful for the business and that have resonance with the stakeholders involved.

2. **Positive language** - The language needs to be positive and inspiring, whilst still being rooted in a narrative that participants can identify with and understand.

3. **Provocative** - It is important to take people out of their normal day-to-day perceptions of their workplace on the basis that 'if you always do what you always did, you will always get what you always got'! Remember that you are trying to prompt for experiences (Discovery) and visions (Dream) that will focus on relatively exceptional moments and aspirations for the future.

4. **Focus on experience or impact** - This is an area that is often not covered in other literature on AI, but is part of current debate, both within AI and other developmental processes (e.g. RBA – Results Based Accountability). Very often there is an exclusive emphasis by AI practitioners on positive experiences. This is valid because it addresses a number of the assumptions of AI (e.g. the language we use creates our reality), however, if taken to the extreme this can lead to a rather limited view of the area of focus. It can also lead to the (false) view that AI ignores the problems within an organisation.

Exploring number 4 above more, if the phrasing of all the Discovery questions focuses on the positive nature of the experience, this can preclude learning that took place during difficult or challenging times. As an example, I was involved in an AI exercise when we were exploring peak learning moments in our lives. During this exercise I had spoken about the death of my father. This was clearly not a positive experience, however, some of the outcomes (on reflection) were very positive and quite profound.

> *"Experience is simply the name we give our mistakes"*
>
> *Oscar Wilde*

So, for me, the suggestion is to consider using language that focuses on the positive nature of the outcome as well as the positive nature of the experience. As an example, look at the two questions below relating to team work.

Q1 – Describe a time when you had an exceptionally positive experience within a team, a time when you really felt highly stimulated and encouraged.

Q2 – Describe a time when you had an exceptionally productive experience within a team, something that ultimately resulted in enhanced communication and working together.

The two examples above would both draw out useful feedback that would form the foundation for later parts of the AI process. The first one does not limit the outcomes (because they are not defined) but does limit the nature of the experience (a positive experience). This can certainly be useful in situations where the desired outcome is not known, or not relatively important.

> *"All men dream, but not equally. Those who dream by night in the dusty recesses of their minds, wake in the day to find that it was vanity: but the dreamers of the day are dangerous men, for they may act on their dreams with open eyes, to make them possible"*
>
> T. E. *Lawrence*

The second question does not define or limit the nature of the experience but does focus on specific desired outcomes. These might have already been identified in the Define Stage as areas that need development. Because the experience has not been labelled as 'positive', it could involve something quite painful at the time, but that resulted in positive outcomes in the short or longer term.

However this is carried out there is always value. If the questions prompt participants to only share good practice or moments of profound learning, this in itself is highly beneficial to the AI process. How often do we get these types of opportunities? How often do we have another person's undivided attention and interest?

Of course some organisations do identify and share good practice. This is either because they want to use it for PR, or to share with others in order to spread the learning. However, interestingly, very few (none that I have worked for) actually spend quality time looking at why and how that good practice occurred – i.e. what the contributory factors were.

So that leads us onto the Discovery Stage of AI. This provides the framework (based on our carefully crafted questions) to allow participants to both share their personal experiences, and the factors that contributed to them.

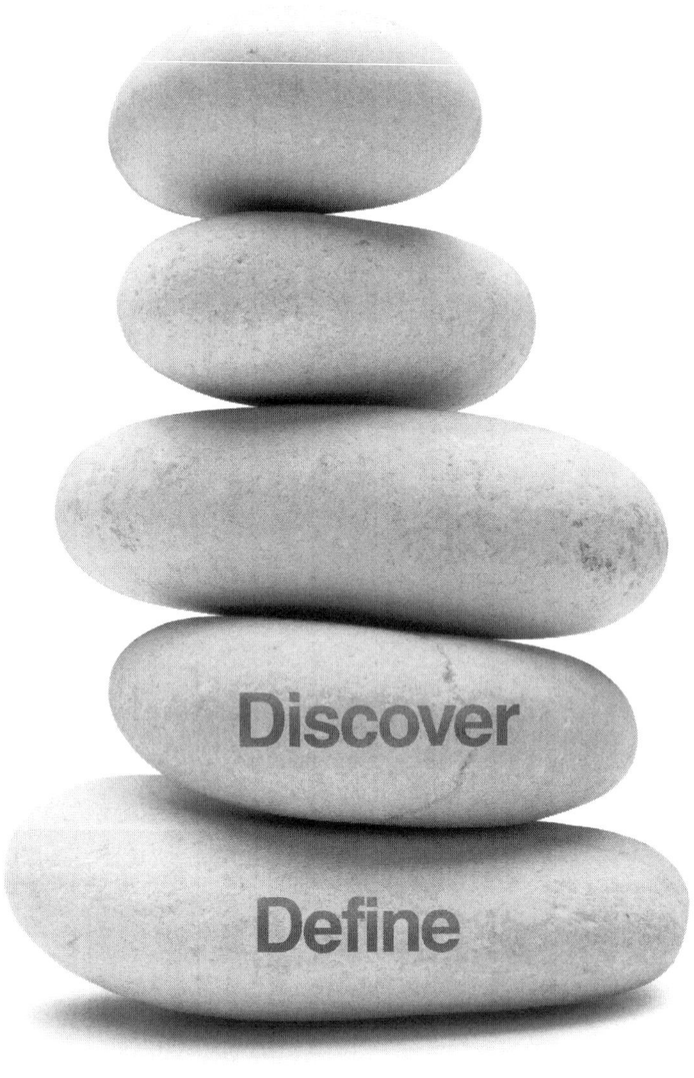
Discover
Define

## Stage 2 - Discover

Discovery is the foundation of AI – it is about identifying and sharing stories and learning based on the real experiences of the key stakeholders within an organisation or group.

The catalysts for the Discovery Stage are the topics agreed in the Define Stage. Topics that are meaningful to the business and the people within it. Topics that are based on issues that need shift and change. Whether this is for reasons to do with culture, systems, processes, environment, or communication etc. The key point here is – the topics need to MATTER to the business and the people within it. If they do not, this is one of the reasons the process can fail to deliver on its potential.

> *"Nothing is so contagious as an example. We never do great good or great evil without bringing about more of the same on the part of others"*
>
> De La Roche Foucauld

So how do we 'do' Discovery? The traditional and tried and trusted method is through one-to-one, face-to-face dialogue. If participants have all come together in a workshop they split into pairs. If they are not in a workshop environment they arrange time together in a quiet space and talk. This all needs planning and will be dependent on a number of factors ranging from logistics (e.g. getting people from diverse locations together) to resources (including possibly paying people for their time).

And what do people talk about? They respond to the questions that have been pre-defined – e.g. 'tell me about a time when you experienced exceptional leadership that inspired others and led to creative solutions... what contributed to that, who was there, how were they behaving, where were you, were any systems or processes involved'? You will notice that in this example there is an emphasis on a positive experience and a positive outcome.

> *"Questions are the creative acts of intelligence"*
>
> Frank Kingdon

You will also notice that there are two elements to the question – the story and the contributory factors. Both are important. The story is the driver, it is the thing that connects the storyteller to the topic – it is real, something they have actually experienced. The reflections on the contributory factors are the building blocks for the rest of the process, the things that will contribute to tangible action plans within the Design and Delivery stages.

If people are in a workshop, they are then brought together into groups. If it is a small workshop (e.g. up to eight people) this could be one group. If it is larger it will be in a number of groups. Ideally the size of the groups should be no less than four and no more than twelve. After the smaller group sessions there is usually a reporting back from each sub-group into the whole group. Clearly the facilitator needs to make some pragmatic decisions on the ground in relation to this reporting process and this will take into consideration the time available for everyone to feed back (both within the initial groupings and to the whole group).

> *"Is there anyone so wise as to learn by the experience of others?"*
>
> *Voltaire*

Taking notes during the pairs work for the Discovery Stage is optional in my view. If people are given the choice they will usually do so. The advantages are clear – it aids the process of feedback, particularly if you have a memory like mine. The main disadvantage is that it can act as a block to the communication. An over emphasis on note taking can certainly distract from the listening process, both for the listener and the teller, there is nothing worse than talking to somebody who has their eyes embedded in a notebook. There is nothing better than good eye contact with verbal and non-verbal feedback. As with most things in life, the answer is usually a happy medium. There is also an option here to consider a role play example. This is not something I have done within AI but it is used a lot within counselling skills training and I think there may be benefits here. Overall, however, there are few strict rules for this (unlike counselling) and my view is that as far as possible just go with the flow during this stage.

> *"Nothing has such power to broaden the mind as the ability to investigate systematically and truly all that comes under thy observation in life"*
>
> *Aurelius, Marcus*

The overall aim here is to slowly distil the essence of the contributory factors from the stories into a common list that has resonance across the total group. If the topic is focused on human interactions, issues like listening, authenticity, honesty, action, usually emerge. If the focus is on systems and processes, issues like clear terms of reference, planning, consultation, feedback, usually emerge. The key point is that whatever emerges comes from participants' direct experiences.

The advantages of getting everyone together in a workshop environment is clear. Everyone receives the same messages and can be 'primed' in terms of the activity and the different roles (i.e. the person telling the story and the person listening). Everyone can then immediately share their stories in groups; identifying common themes in terms of the contributory factors.

However, if this cannot be done for whatever reason, second best is to cascade this stage throughout as much of the organisation as possible, ideally by a core group of people who have had some form of training in the overall process.

This brings us again to different approaches to the delivery of AI. For me the perfect structure is to have everyone together in a workshop for Discovery through to Design and Delivery (this will mean more after further reading). However, if the organisation cannot afford this, the cascade approach needs to be considered.

Above I have referred to a 'core group'. This is a smaller group, selected from within the organisation and wider stakeholder group who have had some AI training and a natural affinity to the AI ethos and thinking. Ideally they will have been through the whole 5D process, but at least have an understanding of the concept and principles. They can then cascade the Discovery questions (and possibly Dream) through the larger organisation over as short a time as practicably possible (dependant on time, geography etc.). Whilst face-to-face meetings are most ideal, less personal approaches are better then nothing – i.e. ensuring everyone has an opportunity to respond. A mix and match is also an option (some face-to-face, some email, questionnaire etc.).

The end game here is to engage as many stakeholders within the Discovery phase as possible, ideally in face-to-face conversations, but if not, then in the best way possible. Remember, some level of engagement is better than no engagement at all.

**Discovery - Why does it work**

I am going to finish off this stage of the AI process by going back and referring to key learnings from the first section of the book – i.e. connecting the practice to the theory.

The Simultaneity Principle of AI asserts that the questions we ask and the stories we share hold the seeds of change. The Discovery Stage is the first opportunity for the wider stakeholder group within the organisation to share these stories, driven by the questions agreed within the Define Stage.

Because these stories centre on positive outcomes (and usually positive experiences), the 'positive psychology' of the group has been established. The Positive Principle and the work of Carl Rogers (underpinned by much wider evidence) asserts that people are innately positive systems and that they respond to positive thoughts and feedback. The Poetic Principle states that we are constantly rewriting and reinterpreting our view of reality: a new view of the reality within the organisation has now been set in motion at the Discovery Stage. This is often referred to in AI as identifying the 'positive core' within an organisational context.

Stacey's work proposes that organisations are highly complex 'organisms' that are based on human systems and interactions which are unpredictable by their very nature. He suggests that organisations need to move toward models of co-creation that involve the people within the organisation. The Discovery Stage of AI lays the foundations for this.

My personal proposition that life is like a jigsaw suggests that learning and understanding has a timeliness. I am proposing that this timeliness actually results in people not being able to understand certain concepts until the time is right – i.e. until they have found the pieces of the jigsaw appropriate to their map of the world first. Carl Rogers' statements around the power and order of experience also support this view.

Because the Discovery Stage starts with people's own experiences – i.e. an actual experience that they have had linked to the topic choice, this automatically has meaning and resonance with them. This is contrary to other traditional training and development approaches that might attempt to offer models and proposals that do not 'fit' into each person's map (jigsaw).

> *"If you want to build a ship, don't drum up people to gather wood, give orders, and divide the work. Rather, teach them to yearn for the far and endless sea"*
>
> *Antoine Saint Exupery*

So now we have the positive core, what is working and what has contributed to that. We will now involve people in perhaps the most exciting and stimulating stage of the AI process – dreaming the dream!

# Dream

# Discover

# Define

## Stage 3 – Dream

The Dream Stage of AI probably seems most familiar to organisations; they often call it visioning. It involves people in looking into the future and creating an image of what the organisation could be like (and potentially be!) given a prescribed set of circumstances. If the organisation is described as going on a journey from A to B, this is B and the Discovery Stage is A.

Where traditional approaches to visioning and the Dream Stage of AI start to part company is in relation to who is involved in the process and how it is delivered. Typically, visioning is carried out by senior managers on away days. A generalised characterisation, but nonetheless fairly accurate. These management teams then return to base with their vision, maybe including an accompanying action plan, and (in some cases) consult with the broader workforce. The plan is then 'SMARTened' up and implemented.

> *"Our demons are our own limitations, which shut us off from realisation of the ubiquity of the spirit... each of these demons is conquered in a vision quest"*
>
> *Joseph Campbell*

More sophisticated organisations then cascade the business plan into the personal development plans of individual staff, usually through structured appraisal and supervision processes. These attempt to identify and designate specific actions into each individual's plan that will support the overarching vision.

The Dream Stage within AI is very different. Firstly, it includes and engages a much broader stakeholder group into the coproduction of the vision. Members of the workforce (and possibly others – e.g. customers, partners etc) come together to create an aspirational future linked to the chosen topics. Again, the importance of the topic choice (decided in the Define Stage) comes through. This can be as narrow as looking at one aspect of the organisation (e.g. leadership, partnership working, customer service, data handling etc), or as wide as a complete organisational review.

> *"Only those who risk going too far can possibly find out how far one can go"*
>
> *T. S. Elliot*

A question is posed that invites participants to imagine that their vision is already in place and to describe what that looks like. For example, if one of the topics was about leadership, the question might ask 'imagine we are 18 months into the future and the organisation has just won a national award for effective leadership – what would that look like'?

This part of the process places people into groups, and my preference is groupings that are multi-disciplinary (i.e. from different departments, roles, responsibilities). Typical group sizes are anything from four (for a small organisation) through to twelve. Even if the total organisation is really large, numbers over twelve (and even this is pushing the limit) usually do not allow for everyone to have the required level of input.

Another relatively unique aspect of the Dream Stage is that creativity is promoted. When I say creativity I mean creative approaches to the sharing and recording of ideas other than a bullet point list of ideas on a sheet of paper (having said that – bulleted lists are OK!). This is often translated into images of some form, but can result in people doing role plays, songs or poems – the options are as varied as the imaginations and confidence of the members of the group.

> *"The faculty of our imagination is both the rudder and the bridle of the senses"*
>
> *Leonardo da Vinci*

Why do we do this? Because creativity is fun and promotes thinking that is outside the box. People remember when they have fun and identify with the results more. In many cases participants will take the results of this stage with them after the process has finished as a reminder of their visions.

There is an important thing to realise about this stage. Visions are driven by three sources.

Firstly, people will draw on things that are already effective and in place, but they want more of. Secondly, people will draw on things that are in place but not working to an adequate level. Thirdly, people will dream of things that are not in place at all, but they think should be. And sometimes this latter type of vision includes things that might be deemed impractical, inappropriate or unrealistic. So let's explore this more.

> *"Without this playing with fantasy no creative work has ever come to birth. The debt we owe to the play of the imagination is incalculable"*
>
> *Carl Jung*

The first type of vision I will label as 'spreading the good practice'. These are things that are working well in the organisation and people would like to see replicated and enhanced more widely. These are often limited to certain teams, or in some cases, specific individuals. In some organisations they are obvious and apparent. In other organisations they are more hidden away and less apparent. However, the bottom line is that many organisations provide few opportunities to identify these (particularly in the latter example) and even fewer provide quality time to analyse why they are occurring.

> "*You see things and say, 'why?' but I dream things that never were and say, 'why not'?"*
>
> *George Bernard Shaw*

The second type I will label as 'improvement'. Those things that might be defined as problems or issues that people would like to see modified, developed or remedied. These are areas that may more typically be identified during a traditional SWOT (Strengths, Weaknesses, Opportunities and Threats) analysis and could drive the action planning process.

The third type I will call 'blue sky thinking', the really creative process that organisations like Apple and Google are so good at. However, again this activity is often restricted to management and delivered in traditional, and dare I say, un-inspirational ways.

The question I always get asked about the Dream Stage is how unrealistic people are 'allowed' to be. Can they really dream the dream? You might think that the obvious response here might be to keep people's aspirations within what might be perceived as the realms of reality. The problem with this of course, is that different people will all have their own perspectives about what constitutes reality – i.e. what is within the realms of possibility.

Imagine if Apple had applied that approach to their entry into the mobile phone market? If their research and development staff had based all their aspirations within what they already knew about or thought was realistic and practical? If you always do what you always did – you always get what you always got!

What Apple did with the iPhone (and some other products) was to totally transform the market, produce something that was truly revolutionary.

However… there is another side to this. There may be situations where some boundaries need to be considered. For example, an organisation may be in a position where it cannot provide additional money for any new projects. In this case it may be appropriate to add this within the question. For example – 'imagine we are 18 months into the future and we have just won an award for the best leadership within the sector, delivered within an environment of no financial increases, what would that look like'.

My view and experience is that it is better not to put any constraints on the dream. The reason? The most important aspect of this part of the process is creative thinking, and most people tend to naturally constrain themselves anyway, without any external influences. The challenge is actually getting them to think out of the box in the first place! And if that concerns you, because you do not want to raise expectations that cannot be fulfilled, I can understand that. But as a very experienced AI trainer once said to me – 'trust the process'. What is important here is that people are given freedom to think as creatively as possible about what could be. Later stages of AI will deal with the practicalities of implementation.

> *"In every block of marble I see a statue as plain as though it stood before me, shaped and perfect in attitude and action. I have only to hew away the rough walls that imprison the lovely apparition to reveal it to the other eyes as mine see it"*
>
> *Michelangelo*

Now, what you might have noticed earlier is that I used that 'dirty' word – problem – i.e. that one catalyst for the Dream Stage is problems or issues that people want to resolve. Of course the whole ethos of AI (if you hadn't already got it) is about using positive language. But that also leads to one of the most common misconceptions and criticisms of the process. So let's deal with that right now...

AI does not ignore problems! It does not ignore them for two reasons.

The first one is dealt with above. During the Dream Stage participants are able to express their perceptions about what the problems and issues are within the organisation – but (and this is key), these are framed in terms of solutions. What we do is totally bypass the conversation about problems and move people directly into solution mode. I have a friend and ex-colleague whose management mantra is 'don't bring me problems just bring me solutions'. This is what the AI process does – it focuses people directly onto the solutions.

Secondly, AI is not a replacement for the need to sort and fix certain problems – not in my world anyway. Let's express it this way. Imagine we (that's you, me and all the other people reading this book at this moment) jump on a plane to Spain tomorrow. We are fed up of sitting in our rooms reading about AI and decide to get a bit of sunshine. We are half way to Spain and one of the engines fails. Would we want the pilot to come back

# The application of AI – Dream

into the cabin and conduct an AI process with us?

You did answer no to that I hope!

So what would we expect the pilot to do? Yup – find the problem as quickly as possible and fix it!

> *"We cannot solve our problems with the same thinking we used when we created them"*
>
> *Albert Einstein*

So there are some very immediate problems that just need sorting within organisations, because if they are not fixed pretty quickly they may have a significant impact on the operation. This might be to do with things (e.g. my PC has just gone down and I have to finish this report by tonight) or they might be to do with people (e.g. one of my staff has been accused of an assault).

Now let's go back to the aeroplane example. The pilot manages to sort the problem and get us to Spain. What might happen next?

Now we are into the zone that is much more about longer term systemic issues. Matters that require more subtle and potentially complex interventions, usually involving people (and how can you get more complex than that?).

The obvious and traditional approach would be to identify the maintenance team who were responsible for that plane at its last scheduled service. We would then review and analyse what happened in detail and apply remedial action. That might range from further training through to reviewing external suppliers and disciplinary action. In ideal circumstances this learning would be communicated throughout all the teams in order to share the mistakes and learn from them.

This 'find the problems and fix them' makes sense and does result in remedial action in relation to the specific problem, but if it is the only strategy the organisation takes it is missing one big 'trick'. What is being missed are the teams within the organisation who have a 0% (or close) error record. What is it they are doing that enables them to work so effectively as individuals and teams? What processes and systems are in place? What type of physical environment is supporting this? SO much potential learning!

And then once we have discovered this, let's bring all the teams together with other layers of the organisation. Maybe let's involve some of our main suppliers as one of the key stakeholders in this quality debate. Let's all dream about what it might look like if our company had just won an industry award for safety. Let's really think out of the proverbial box about how we could work in creative and innovative ways to become that high performing organisation!

**Dream – why does it work?**

Like Discovery, the Dream Stage of AI is characterised mainly by the depth and width of its stakeholder involvement.

In terms of depth, all layers of the organisation are involved, from senior managers through to front-line workers. Everybody contributes to the dream, adding their unique perspective in terms of experience and knowledge. Employees at the front-line very often have the answers that many organisations pay highly paid consultants to provide. Actually, what is the first thing that many of those highly paid consultants do when reviewing an organisation? Yep – they talk to the staff doing the job. What the consultants usually bring to the table, however, is the ability to take that information and make something of it – make connections, make judgements and then ultimately make recommendations. What the AI process does is all that and more – i.e. it engages representatives of the whole organisation in making its own recommendations and, most critically, engages them in taking ownership of the actions.

> *"There are those who look at things the way they are, and ask why... I dream of things that never were, and ask why not?*
>
> *Robert Kennedy*

Secondly, in relation to 'width', the Dream Stage involves those wider stakeholders, the customers, service users, partners, suppliers etc. All these people bring more 'tangential' perspectives to the dream, new ways of looking at things from their own unique perspective. And the important point here is that these people could never have been involved if a traditional review was conducted. Would any company involve these people in a process of hanging out their dirty laundry? What the Dream process does is very cleverly reframe this into a dialogue about 'let's look at what the laundry might look like when it's clean – in fact when it is the cleanest you have ever seen it'!

> *"You wish to see; Listen.*
> *Hearing is a step towards Vision"*
>
> *St. Bernard*

The other key aspect of the Dream Stage that is different from most visioning exercises is the addition of the fun factor. Some visioning exercises might involve this, but my experience is that most don't. By encouraging people to be creative with their images of the future, they are further engaged with the process. Why? Because nothing aids the learning and creative process like having fun.

# The application of AI – Design

**Design**

**Dream**

**Discover**

**Define**

## Stage 4 – Design

Now we have the 'meat' of the process. Through Discover and Dream we have examples of what is working – and why. We also have aspirations of the future which embrace those issues and problems that people had – but framed in terms of solutions. So what do we do with this?

What we do is Design. We again involve those participants in the process of adapting and 'honing' this information into some form of action plan. One of the Wikipedia definitions of Design is 'a roadmap or a strategic approach for someone to achieve a unique expectation. It defines the specifications, plans, parameters, costs, activities, processes and how and what to do within legal, political, social, environmental, safety and economic constraints in achieving that objective'. You will note that within this definition there is a very strong reference to parameters; practical influencers and boundaries that we have to work within. This is also the stage of AI that seeks to maintain a balance between the creative ideas and some level of pragmatism.

> *"If you only care enough for a result, you will almost certainly attain it"*
>
> *William James*

This is one of the challenges of the process and takes sensitivity and skill. Whilst the Discovery information is rooted in real experience, the outcomes from the Dream Stage can be just that – dreams. Earlier I shared my view that people need to be given permission to dream the dream. At the Design Stage we start to take people into the world of pragmatic responses, without losing the essence and energy created earlier. A very 'delicate' and sensitive process. One of the ways we do this is through the use of Provocative Propositions.

### Provocative Propositions

This is a phrase that, to my knowledge, is unique to AI – i.e. it emerged from the development of the AI approach and the 4/5D process. It is often referred to as the bridge between Dream and Design. It attempts to manage that balance between blue sky thinking and pragmatism. Not easy!

The name sort of gives it away – Provocative Propositions. One definition of provocative is – 'serving or tending to provoke, excite, or stimulate; stimulating discussion or exciting controversy'. The key thing here is that something provocative gets a reaction, it usually challenges the norm and makes us take notice.

Within the 5D Cycle Provocative Propositions follow some rules and these rules seek to balance what might be perceived as unrealistic aspirations with some element of appropriateness and practicality to the context (i.e. the focus of the topic within the organisational context). Getting this balance right is one of the elements of AI that requires real judgement. Get it wrong in one direction and new possibilities are lost. Get it wrong in the other and the more pragmatic participants will start to disengage. Don't forget, we have already encouraged people to think in a liberated fashion in the Dream Stage. Ideas should have already emerged that have taken people outside their normal boundaries.

Let's explore the guidelines for writing Provocative Propositions; are they...

- Provocative – do they stretch, challenge or interrupt?

- Positive – are they written in positive terms?

- Grounded – are there examples that demonstrate the proposition as a real possibility?

- Desired – if pursued, would the organisation and the people in it connect with the proposition – would they want it?

- Written in the current tense – is it written as if it is in place now?

The development of provocative propositions is one of the elements of the 5D process that can be optional. A decision on this is based on two considerations. Firstly time. If you have limited time (e.g. attempting to cover the process in a day) I would drop PPs before anything else. Secondly, the nature of the outcomes from the Dream Stage. In some cases the aspirations articulated during this stage are already effectively written as PPs, that may either result in a shortened PP process or a decision that they are not needed at all.

> "Our doubts are traitors and make us lose the good we oft might win by fearing to attempt"
>
> *Shakespeare*

Don't get me wrong, overall I am a fan of this stage, it concentrates the mind, makes people prioritise, and results in statements that are effectively mission statements (around a theme). They are also one of the parts of the process that can be physically captured and taken away as reference points, reminding people in a very succinct and targetted way of their aspirations. I have worked with a number of organisations where these have been framed and put on the office walls.

The best way to develop provocative propositions is in groups, similar to the Dream Stage. Group sizes should be approximately the same (i.e. four to twelve) and membership is not critical. However, in my view it again makes sense to try and ensure some level of 'depth' (layers of the organisation) and 'width' (stakeholders – if present).

So, onto the Design Stage proper. This involves agreeing actions that build on key elements of the Discovery Stage to deliver on the aspirations set out in the Dream. These aspirations may or may not be crystallised by the development of PPs.

> *"The best way to predict the future is to create it"*
>
> Peter Drucker

It is done in groups, either the same as the PP groups or by specialism, interest or team. Like all options the decision on group makeup is a double-edged sword. Cross fertilisation ensures a wide range of knowledge and experience is brought to bear on each area of focus. Grouping by specialism or team ensures an alignment of interests that may ensure the process moves forwards more quickly and efficiently.

To throw another variable into the mix, this is the stage that I find lends itself to another powerful approach called Open Space Technology (OST). OST is a complete process in itself and books have been written on the subject, the best of which (in my view) is by the

> *"Design is not just what it looks like and feels like. Design is how it works"*
>
> Steve Jobs

originator - Harrison Owen. The essence of OST is that it allows for a self organising process within a group, enabling people who have a passion for a particular topic to take a lead in that area and for others to contribute to discussions on a range of topics in a very flexible manner.

In relation to using OST during the Design Stage of AI, I will ask for volunteers to lead on specific topic areas that arise out of the Dream Stage or PP process. These will naturally be people who have a particular interest or passion for a topic or theme. These people will then set themselves up at tables and the remaining participants are invited to join them as and when they wish. The result is that people drift from table to table based on their involvement and interest. This is an extremely liberating and efficient way of conducting dialogue. How many meetings have you been to where you felt you would like to leave before the end, usually because you feel you have contributed all you need to contribute, or you have heard all you need to hear?

The use of OST usually needs time and space (i.e. physical space), but if you have both of these I would highly recommend it during the Design Stage.

Another variable to throw into the mix at the Design Stage are Design Elements. These are aspects of the design process that are predetermined in order to provide some guidelines and structure for the action planning. Some examples of these Design Elements include:

o Business process

o Communication systems and processes

o Culture

o Customer / client relationships

o Education / training / CPD

o Leadership

o Management practices

o Policies and procedures

o Values

o Social responsibility

o Sustainability

o Strategy

o Structures

o Systems

o Technology

o Relationships

o Governance structures

o Knowledge management systems

o Public relations

o Practices and principles

o Power and authority

o Project management

One way to structure people's thinking at this stage is to present the desired design elements within a Fishbone layout, this is based on Kaoru Ishikawa's concept (see next page).

Zen and the Art of Appreciative Inquiry

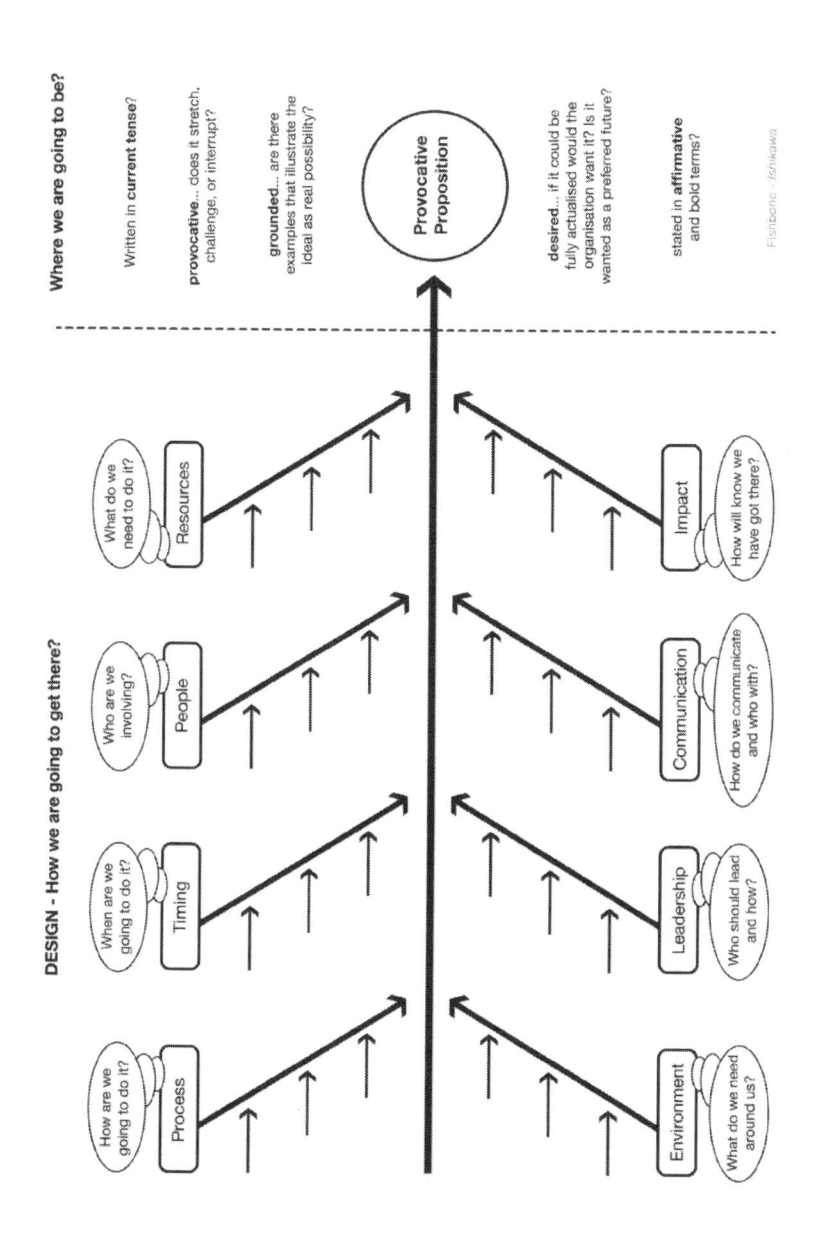

**Where we are going to be?**

Written in **current tense**?

**provocative**... does it stretch, challenge, or interrupt?

**grounded**... are there examples that illustrate the ideal as real possibility?

**desired**... if it could be fully actualised would the organisation want it? Is it wanted as a preferred future?

stated in **affirmative** and bold terms?

Provocative Proposition

**DESIGN - How we are going to get there?**

- How are we going to do it? — Process
- When are we going to do it? — Timing
- Who are we involving? — People
- What do we need to do it? — Resources
- What do we need around us? — Environment
- Who should lead and how? — Leadership
- How do we communicate and who with? — Communication
- How will know we have got there? — Impact

Fishbone - *Ishikawa*

81

How much you decide to steer people's thinking at the Design Stage is one of the many variables within the process that needs consideration. As with many decisions there are pros and cons. The main advantage is that it focuses people's minds very quickly and possibly opens up new avenues for them to follow. The main disadvantage is that it takes away some of the spontaneity and 'self growth' within the group – i.e. it doesn't allow them to think about and discover these elements themselves.

Another aspect of the process that may need to be introduced at this stage and others, is prioritisation. It is nearly always the case that participants produce lots and lots of ideas during the middle 3Ds (Discover, Dream and Design). This results in pages and pages of flip-chart paper all around the room. The ideas on the paper will have resulted from the views of one or two people, through to those that will have been common to most or all of the group. All these ideas are valid because it may just be that one idea from one person could be the catalyst for the most momentous change and improvement. However, once all these ideas are 'out there' for the whole group to consider, it may be that some form of prioritisation is required.

This most often occurs at the Design Stage, either in relation to the Provocative Propositions or when high level actions are agreed. This prioritisation is normally based on what is perceived as the most important issues in relation to the organisation's mission, those that will have most impact on the bottom line, whether that be related to a product or service. Another consideration is that in any programme of change quick wins are required, actions that can be put into practice as soon as possible so that participants can see the fruits of their work.

One of the best ways to get people involved in this prioritisation is through the use of a voting system based on sticky dots. I normally give each participant a line of about 10 dots to use as they wish. For example, if the group comes up with a list of 9 PPs, I invite each person to use their dots to indicate their view of the 'weighting' in terms of importance of each PP. One person may decide to use all 10 dots on one PP. Another may spread them amongst 4 etc. If the dots are used against the actions that come out of the Design Stage they might have to prioritise amongst 30 or 40 (or more) actions – this is fairly typical of the number of actions that will arise from the process.

> *"Business, more than any other occupation, is a continual dealing with the future; it is a continual calculation, an instinctive exercise in foresight"*
>
> Henry R. Luce

The last thing to say about actions from the Design Stage is that it is rare that these are fully SMART (specific, measurable, achievable, realistic and time-scaled). The process should produce actions that tick the 'achievable' and 'realistic' boxes, but it is usual that more work needs to be carried out on wording to ensure they are fully 'specific', 'measurable', and 'time-scaled'. However, there is rarely enough time to do this within the larger AI process and it is not generally appropriate to involve a large number of people in this detailed work. The important thing is that everyone has had a hand in designing the main thrust of movement and feel energy and ownership for this. This will include people taking actual ownership of specific actions – this naturally occurs if the Open Space methodology has been used (i.e. people volunteer to lead discussions on the areas of focus or PPs).

This leads us to the final stage, putting ideas and plans into action, delivering on our intention.

# The application of AI – Deliver

## Stage 5 – Deliver

This last Stage of the AI process is referred to as either Deliver or Destiny. I generally use the word Delivery (if I actually label it in any way during the process – not essential!) because it is more accessible and understandable. However, Destiny is more subtle and interesting and can stimulate deeper thinking and conversations about how we can go beyond traditional planning processes.

Deliver, traditionally focused on taking the outcomes of the Design Stage (actions) forward and firming them up in terms of implementation strategies. It also acknowledged the importance of sustainability, the challenge of 'doing the thing you said you would do, long after the mood you said it in has passed'. I often refer to this as the 'holiday romance' syndrome - that feeling of being in a land far, far away with lots of sunshine and no work pressures, only to be flown back to 'reality' and the pressures that go along with this. This is why many change and development strategies fail, and why training, away days and developmental workshops become like a distant dream. And this is why the Delivery Stage is important.

> *"There are costs and risks to a program of action, but they are far less than the long range risk and costs of comfortable inaction"*
>
> *John F. Kennedy*

There are reasons why the actions from the AI process naturally have more chance of follow-through and success than more traditional processes, regardless of the Delivery Stage. These have been stressed throughout this book, but include 'starting from where people are at' through the Discovery Stage. 'Engaging people in creative visioning' through the Dream Stage. And 'prioritising agreed actions' through the Design Stage. Essentially all key stakeholders are involved in the whole 'A to B' process, have fun doing it, and take ownership of the resultant actions.

However, over and above the natural energy that is created through AI, the Delivery Stage attempts to consolidate this energy and jointly agree strategies that will make the whole process sustainable. The seeds of these strategies are normally discussed at the AI Summit (i.e. all stakeholders together in a workshop environment) but then carried through into the day-to-day workplace.

> *"I'm a great believer in luck, and I find the harder I work, the more I have of it"*
>
> *Thomas Jefferson*

The nature of the strategies obviously cannot be pre-determined. As with the rest of the AI process participants are encouraged to be creative and realistic about these, but the actual range of options is as limitless as people's imagination and knowledge. This will range from task and finish groups through to embedding the AI thinking and process itself into the organisation. In fact, some studies have shown that those organisations that do the latter are the ones that succeed most in sustaining the change and improvement.

One good example is a study by Martin Stellnberger (Victoria University of Wellington 2010) that looked at three large-scale AI interventions (between 130 and 320 participants in the summit) within three organisations operating in the banking and service industries. The research showed that whilst interviewees across all three organisations shared positive views and feelings about the process, the longer term impact was variable. Two out of three organisations appeared to have underestimated the importance of what should happen after the event and ultimately failed in demonstrating significant benefits following the AI summit. In contrast, the third organisation put a strong emphasis on planning actions that followed the summit and integrated AI into their operations.

To expand on this last point, the third organisation (Org 1 in the study) felt it important to feed AI into organisational processes not just projects. They facilitated weekly employee engagement meetings to integrate AI thinking into the day-to-day work of all their staff and this was linked to relevant business topics and issues.

Within the other two organisations (Orgs 2 and 3) projects tended to 'fall over' quickly and the outcomes were to a great extent unsatisfactory'. Also, people who were not part of the process remained apart and for them AI remained or become irrelevant.

In addition, putting an emphasis on projects created the perception that there was an end to the projects and the AI thinking. Putting an emphasis on integrating AI processes produced sustained activity and results.

In another paper by Gervase R. Bushe – 'When is Appreciative Inquiry Transformational? A Meta-Case Analysis', 20 cases of using AI for transformational change were examined. Although all adhered broadly to the 4/5D Cycle, only seven (35%) showed transformational outcomes. The paper asserts that 'In 83% of the transformational cases, the destiny or action phase of the AI was best characterised as improvisational. In contrast, 83% of the non-transformational cases used more standard implementation approaches to the action phase in which attempts were made to implement centrally agreed upon targets and plans'.

The author concluded that 'these two qualities of appreciative inquiry, a focus on changing how people think instead of what people do, and a focus on supporting self-organising change processes that flow from new ideas rather than leading implementation of centrally or consensually agreed upon changes, appear to be key contributions of AI to the theory and practice of large systems change that merit further study and elaboration'.

## Summary

The practical application of the 5D model is not complicated in concept.

**Define** what you are going to do and what you are going to focus on - the topic choice. Include as many stakeholders in this process as possible including depth (levels of the organisation) and breadth (as wide a range of stakeholders as possible – internal and external).

**Discover** what is working and why, based around the topic choice. This is based on participants' real experiences, ideally within the organisation. Start to change the nature of the conversations that take place within the organisation.

**Dream** about the future – paint a 'picture' of the organisation in an identified period of time, again, with a focus on the topic choice. In most cases allow people to be truly aspirational at this stage.

**Design** what you are going to do to deliver on your aspirations. Building on the best of current practice and balancing the competing elements of ideas being grounded in reality without losing opportunities to keep your mind open to new possibilities.

**Deliver** on what you said you were going to do (long after the mood you said it in has passed!). Engage participants in developing ideas about how this can be achieved and embed AI thinking into future ways of working. Change the conversations that occur in the organisation and the culture and levels of commitment will change too!

*The overwhelming majority of facts, the sights and sounds that are around us every second and the relationships among them and everything in our memory - these have no Quality, in fact they have negative Quality. If they were all present at once our consciousness would be so jammed with meaningless data we couldn't think or act. So we preselect on the basis of Quality, or, to put it Phaedrus' way, the track of Quality preselects what data we're going to be conscious of, and it makes this selection in such a way as to best harmonize what we are with what we are becoming.*

*Robert M Pirsig – Zen and the Art of Motorcycle Maintenance*

# 5. DOES IT WORK?

The million dollar question! There are so many theories 'out there' that make a multitude of claims, mostly in relation to personal or organisational development, or both. These then lie alongside those that describe the perfect manager or even the meaning of life!

The authors of these theories have generally done one thing very well. They have expertly re-packaged one or more previous theories in a way that resonates with us in some way. They have then managed to gain that critical point of self momentum that drives them forwards on a self-sustaining trajectory towards relative fame and fortune.

These theories fall into one of two broad categories, they have some real substance or they are like the Emperor's New Clothes. In the latter example people (and organisations) get caught in the wave of enthusiasm. 'All these people can't be wrong – can they?' Human resource departments commit the organisation to this or that particular theory and bring in one of the growing army of consultants that jump onto the proverbial bandwagon. Money is spent and changes are again made (because inevitably this change will be one of many over the years). The organisation then commits to this latest fad until... you got it. The next new 'latest' breakthrough climbs to the top of the charts and claims to fix the organisation's latest set of 'ills' and challenges (and

> *"No way of thinking or doing, however ancient, can be trusted without proof. Whatever everybody echoes or in silence passes by as true today may turn out to be falsehood tomorrow, mere smoke of opinion, which some had trusted for a cloud that would sprinkle fertilizing rain on their fields"*
>
> *Henry David Thoreau.*

they will always be there).

It might be at this point that you are thinking – 'is AI any different'? Well, to be completely objective, to some degree probably not. It is a set of theories and related practice that can be tracked back to a range of other theories and practices, mostly rooted in the Positive Psychology movement attributed to Martin Seligman. Undoubtedly we could then make other links to proponents of other theories and this could go on and on. What each person has successfully done is make connections and package and promote these connections effectively.

So let's return to the initial question – does it work, and if it does, what makes it different to all those other fads that have come and gone over the years? The answer – a very Zen-like yes and no.

Let me take you back to my airplane analogy. The plane has a potentially catastrophic fault, do we want to carry out an AI exercise? No, we just want to find the problem and fix it as quickly as possible. However, we may then want to apply AI in order to correct longer term systemic issues that led to the problem in the first place. There are many issues within the workplace that fit the same profile. We may need to dismiss a particular member of staff following a series of disciplinary issues, or one incident of gross misconduct. However, we may then be able to use an AI process in order to introduce new ways of doing things that minimises the possibility of that event recurring with other members of the workforce.

> *"If we knew what it was we were doing, it would not be called research, would it"?*
>
> *Albert Einstein*

Setting aside this difference – does AI work? OK– I'm still going to resist providing a straight yes or no answer.

In my view, anything 'works' if it accomplishes what it sets out to do. It all comes back to what you wanted from it in the first place, which is of course, why it is so important to know what you want in the first place!

> *"The outcome of any serious research can only be to make two questions grow where only one grew before"*
>
> *Thorstein Veblen*

Let's get into the realms of objectivity and subjectivity. If my aim is to make the company 'more successful', that is a subjective measure and too broad. In some people's minds success might mean following an ethical stance, in others (e.g. local government) it might be the quality and reach (i.e. the numbers of people who receive the service) of the services it provides. And here we start to get to the crux of the issue – the difference between qualitative and quantitative evaluation.

Qualitative evaluation is based on the viewpoint of the person or people making the evaluation. Because it is based on the view of the subject (the person making the judgement) it is deemed to be subjective. This whole area of subjective perception is the backbone of AI and the Social Constructionist theory – i.e. that our perceptions of the world are made up of our subjective viewpoints 'layered' with the interactions we have with others on a daily basis. Because of this, we (and the organisations we work for) are constantly re-writing our view of ourselves and everything around us.

AI 'exploits' this central assertion of Social Constructionism in order to engage as many people operating within the system (organisation in this case) in constructing a new and jointly owned reality. In other words the 5D process engages participants in a dialogue that takes them from their current 'place' in the organisational jigsaw (via the Discovery Stage) to a jointly held vision of the future. The process creates a conducive environment for this dialogue to occur in order to bring people to this new shared perception.

> *"Education is not filling a bucket but lighting a fire"*
>
> *Yeats*

However, in relation to a critical evaluation of the effectiveness of AI, any form of qualitative analysis is generally bound to be positive in its nature – i.e. people are usually going to report positively on how engaged they feel in the process and how much ownership they have of the outcomes from the Design Stage. This, in many ways, is not a bad thing, but it is important to realise the limitations and boundaries of this type of evaluation. I will say more about this later.

Quantitative evaluation on the other hand focuses on numeric data that has an objective truth about it – i.e. if I give two people a piece of wood and ask them both to measure the wood with the same tape measure we will get the same result. Similarly, if our definition of success within an AI intervention is the production rate of workers on a production line, this is far more objective – i.e. if you asked 10 people to count the numbers of widgets coming off the end of the line at the end of the day they would all give the same answer (presuming they could all count, didn't fall asleep etc!).

Now comes the problem. It isn't that easy is it? Taking our assembly line example, how do we know that another factor didn't come into play apart from the AI intervention? Maybe there were differences in the way the assembly line itself operated that day. Maybe there was one person off sick who used to talk incessantly and put the other workers off their work. Maybe the boss visited and actually asked workers how they were feeling that day! And so it goes on.

The reality is, within the field of human dynamics (and that is generally what we are talking about in relation to AI), it is virtually impossible to carry out any tests that conclusively evidence the effectiveness of the intervention. Even if control groups are established (i.e. another group or groups that do not receive the intervention) the same variables can still come into play.

So – do we give up on our search for validation of the effectiveness of AI? No, that would not be sensible; the point is we need to be aware of the limitations of any research that is carried out in this area (or virtually any other similar area). In particular we need to be cautious of 'evidence' from the people who have facilitated the process.

> *"As you navigate through the rest of your life, be open to collaboration. Other people and other people's ideas are often better than your own. Find a group of people who challenge and inspire you, spend a lot of time with them, and it will change your life"*
>
> *Amy Poehler*

Hold on, you might say, doesn't that include you? You are writing this book as a proponent of AI and providing us with very subjective evidence from your own experiences and perspective.

Yes, I will say. You are right. However, I am attempting to provide you with as much information as possible in order for you to come to your own conclusions based on your own experiences and that of others.

Let me return to the work of Gervase R. Bushe. I referred in the last section to his paper 'When is Appreciative Inquiry Transformational? A Meta-Case Analysis'. This focuses on the effectiveness of the Delivery / Destiny Stage in producing 'real' transformation within an organisation. One of the main assertions in this paper is that if we want to go beyond 'just another' action planning process we need to think in more creative ways about how we carry out the AI process. In particular we need to focus more on changing how people think rather than what they do.

This again brings me back to the fact that 'does it work' is reliant on knowing what you want from the process in the first place. For example, if what you want is a truly transformational change within an organisation you need to be very clear about this from the start and ensure that everyone is signed up to, and understands, what and who this will involve. Very often this requires an explicit commitment from senior managers to supporting post-intervention activity – i.e. changes to the way the organisation does things based on AI thinking and methodology.

But what if we have 'lower level' aspirations for the process. What if we want to fully engage the workforce and other stakeholders in a process of change and development within an organisation that leads to a business plan that everybody buys into. Bushe makes the argument that other processes (other than AI) can possibly do this equally as well. However, based on my own experience (of inspecting organisations against their own self-assessment processes), none that I am aware of do it as well as AI. This is for reasons that are fully articulated throughout this book – i.e. the full engagement of key stakeholders in all parts of the journey from A to B. I would also argue that this type of smaller scale exercise is actually not easy to achieve – again, finding out where A and B are is relatively easy; taking people with you is the hard part!

I would now like to move on to one of Bushe's other papers - 'A comparative case study of appreciative inquiries in one organization: implications for practice'. I focus on Bushe because he is one of the few people I have found 'out there' at the moment who is conducting any form of relatively robust critical analysis of the AI process.

> *"The only thing that interferes with my learning is my education"*
>
> *Albert Einstein*

During this research, Bushe reviewed the implementation of an AI intervention across eight different education sites within a Canadian urban school district. The title of the inquiry was 'what do we know about learning'. Data collected over the following year indicated that four of the sites experienced transformational changes, two sites had incremental changes and two showed little or no change.

### Findings within the four transformational sites
o   A marked jump in student engagement spurred by the experience of student engagement in the inquiry;

- The AI process appeared to inject new life and vitality and a number of innovative projects aimed at making the school more attractive to new students ensued;

- A transformation in the level of collaboration amongst teachers in different disciplines leading to new cross-disciplinary course offerings, informal mentoring of new teachers, new collaboration between teachers and support staff;

- A breakthrough in relations between the high school and the five elementary schools that feed into it;

**Findings within the sites with incremental changes**
- Some success with increasing cross curricular activities, social responsibility efforts amongst students and gaining funding for a "green project" (but the school had been pursuing all of these activities prior to the AI);

- Some increase in the level of collaboration of the adult learning centre in their catchment area and a number of small projects aimed at community partnerships (but the centre already had a reputation for being ahead of others in the level of collaboration among schools and level of community partnerships);

**Findings within the sites with no change**
- A high school/elementary school combination where the AI had no discernible impact on the high school and perhaps some incremental effects on the elementary school;

- A single high school where there were negative descriptions of the AI effort, mostly to do with it being a waste of time and resources.

The full paper by Bushe (which is worth reading) describes a relatively thorough analysis of the interventions and the background context in terms of introduction, delivery, and analysis. In summary the findings from the work concluded that:

- The level of engagement and passion of the principals in each site was a fairly strong predictor of change;

- Sites with no change were significantly worse at including the right people in the inquiry or the summit, given the focus chosen for the inquiry;

- There was some relationship between the skills, effectiveness and credibility of internal change agents and level of change (site coordinators, active site committee members);
- Sites where there were no identified problems that the AI was attempting to solve either had no change or incremental change;
- By and large, the more effort leaders put into integrating the results of the summit back into their schools, the more change observed;
- The Appreciative Inquiry was successful at increasing student engagement and empowerment where increasing student empowerment was a priority for school administrators;
- The Appreciative Inquiry was successful at building relationships between groups that participated together in it;
- The Appreciative Inquiry increased distributed leadership in most of the sites;
- The Appreciative Inquiry process had transformational effects beyond the sites themselves;
- The level of positive affect generated by the inquiry was not a predictor of the level of change;
- The study highlights that many of the normal organisation development processes required for successful change are required for appreciative inquiry as well. AI does not magically overcome poor leadership, communication failures, and unresolved conflicts.

## Does it work, does it make a difference – summing up

Let me repeat some things I said earlier, whether AI works is dependent on two things. Firstly – it depends on how well you do it. Secondly – it depends on how you define 'making a difference'.

In the worst case scenario you can attempt to create transformational change and do it very badly – i.e. you can have very demanding aims and objectives and totally underestimate what that type of change demands. Result – failure!

In the best case scenario you can be very clear and realistic about your aims and objectives (hence the critical importance of the Define Stage) and do it very well. Result – success!

I know the above two conclusions are obvious but they need stating. So now let's explore what 'doing it well' consists of.

*Stop this day and night with me and you shall possess the origin of all poems,*
*You shall possess the good of the earth and sun, (there are millions of suns left,)*
*You shall no longer take things at second or third hand, nor look through the eyes of the dead, nor feed on the spectres in books,*
*You shall not look through my eyes either, nor take things from me,*
*You shall listen to all sides and filter them from yourself.*

*Walt Whitman – extract from Song of Myself*

# 6. DOING IT WELL – KEY ELEMENTS

Doing 'it' well will be contingent on a wide range of variables that are almost endless. I am therefore not even going to attempt to name them all. There are obvious ones like the competence of the facilitator, through to not so obvious ones like the psychology of the group you are working with based on experiences of previous interventions. However, here are my list of things that nearly always need to be borne in mind before taking that first step onto the AI path.

1. **Identify your core group for delivery**. This will range from one person (internal or external) in small scale interventions through to an extended group. These might be people who are already familiar and experienced with AI or a group that is up-skilled to jointly deliver the process. This concept of up-skilling a core group within the organisation is appealing due to cost, sustainability and personal development considerations.

   > "The people who get on in this world are the people who get up and look for the circumstances they want, and, if they can't find them, make them"
   >
   > George Bernard Shaw

2. **Define the task** – like any project clarity of purpose is paramount. People need to have a clear idea about the purpose of the exercise and the intended outcomes (what difference will it make to whom). In most cases, the further you can link the outcomes (or at least some of them) to the end user (there is always an end user – internal or external) the better. The explicit purpose and outcomes then ultimately define whether the project has been successful or not. If, on one end of the scale, all you want to do is effectively engage a wide range of stakeholders in some form of consultation exercise, your definition of success may be as

simple as numbers attending, observed levels of engagement, supportive evaluation sheets and tangible ideas, views and comments from your stakeholder groups. If, on the other hand, you want to take the whole organisation through a process of transformation and/or culture change, you will need performance indicators that span both the immediate and long term (to indicate sustained change and improvement).

3. **Define the topics and word them well** – the topics (linking to the purpose and outcome) are the catalyst for the whole AI process. Get them right and you have sown the seeds of success. Get them wrong and you have missed a critical opportunity to engage people on a journey that is meaningful and relevant to the business. If you are attempting to respond to problematic issues within the organisation or group, make sure you identify those correctly, or allow space for them to be identified by others within the process. The 'agenda' in terms of what is problematic will nearly always initially come from management, because they are generally the catalyst for these types of interventions. However, you need to ensure that the views of participants are factored in. One simple way to do this is to ask all people the three wishes question – i.e. if you had three wishes about the future of this organisation, group, product or service etc – what would they be? It is incredible how informative such a simple question can be.

> *"In a world that is constantly changing, there is no one subject or set of subjects that will serve you for the foreseeable future, let alone for the rest of your life. The most important skill to acquire now is learning how to learn"*
>
> *John Naisbitt*

4. **Get the logistics right.** AI is like any other training and development type activity. It needs planning well in terms of logistics. This includes communications to participants, time allocation, venue and environment (including space), transport, replacement cover, etc.

5. **Ensure 'depth'.** Ensure you have people at as many levels of the organisation or group as possible. This includes decision makers and front-line workers. Miss either end of the scale and the process will be weakened.

6. **Ensure 'width'.** Ensure you have as wide a range of stakeholders as possible who have an interest (of any type) in the focus of the AI exercise. This may include workers from other sections, partner organisations, customers, service users, suppliers, etc. All my

experiences, and those of others, supports this view virtually without exception. And the key element that allows this to take place is the positive focus and framing of AI – i.e. the organisation or group is not overtly hanging its 'dirty washing' out to dry. But remember, problems ARE addressed, just within a positive, solution based focus.

7. **Allow people time** - particularly during the Discovery Stage to fully explore and share the contributory factors of the stories of peak practice or outcomes. Also ensure they understand the value of exploring this and 'drilling down' to the wealth of information that can emerge. Also recognise that there are some skills in doing this and consider some form of exploration of these skills with participants.

8. **'Permit' creative thinking and feedback** - particularly during the Dream Stage. Also stress the importance of having fun (although given the right environment people will tend to do this anyway). Also permit people to dream the dream. The question will usually get asked about how realistic they should be – encourage them not to be restricted by boundaries. This is important because people will naturally tend to be realistic and the next stage of the process deals with this anyway. If truly transformational change is required, in terms of how people work or what they produce (think iPhone), blue sky thinking needs to be encouraged.

9. **Consider the use of Provocative Propositions and generally use them**. They are a useful way to design statements that are generative and are a catalyst and reminder over the longer term.

10. **Encourage and support people to think beyond just producing action plans** in response to identified issues (although these are an important outcome of the process). Try to get them to think about how they think as well as what they do. New mindsets should have been generated through the process and this needs exploring in terms of wider application within the organisation.

So now we know what we need to do, or the critical elements anyway. The next question is, how do we know if we have succeeded?

# 7. MEASURING SUCCESS

To measure success in relation to any intervention you need to know what you want from the process – the outcomes and/or outputs. If you don't know what success looks like you will never know if you have achieved it.

However… there is a caveat here – do not become obsessive over this. I have seen this happen over and over again in relation to the work I do, particularly within local government and other not-for-profit organisations. People get so hyped up over defining and measuring outcomes that this becomes the dominant activity. Not only this, but there is ongoing confusion between outcomes and outputs and people spend their lives trying to clarify this within the larger workforce, often without success. In other words, much of the organisation's limited resource is dedicated to this activity, to the detriment of the actual delivery of the service! Within an AI context, what this can also do is blind you to other solutions that 'magically' emerge during the process; solutions that could turn out to be more important than your original focus. As somebody once said to me – 'plan hard, hang loose'.

> *"To raise new questions, new possibilities, to regard old problems from a new angle, requires creative imagination and marks real advance in science"*
>
> *Albert Einstein*

Having said this, it is critical to be clear about what it is you want from the intervention exercise. The AI process can be used in a range of ways (see next section), but everyone needs to be clear about the purpose and the 'end game'. How and if to measure this is the challenge and dilemma.

I am going to be controversial here and suggest you don't get too hung up over whether you want an outcome or an output, or if the data is quantitative or qualitative! Just be clear what it is you want and drill down so this is as close to your end product or bottom line as possible. For example if you are a business, your bottom line is generally profit. If you are a local government department your bottom line is usually impact on your customers – the population within your area of remit. So when I use the term outcome I am going to define this as the 'the desired end result of what you do'; has it made a difference.

Let's look at two extremes in terms of use of the AI process, some of this is expanded on in the next section.

You may only want to use AI as an 'engagement tool', and the level of engagement is an end in itself (although there will inevitably be other success criteria that follow). For example, you have been trying to get the views and ideas of disparate groups of stakeholders for many years but have never really managed to get them engaged in the process in any sort of meaningful way. You may even have had feedback to say that the process was tokenistic – a common criticism of consultation events with stakeholder groups.

Typically, consultation with stakeholders can consist of, "this is what we have decided, what do you think?" Why do people think this is tokenistic? Because the decisions have usually already been made and the people consulting are often going through a superficial process. It is not necessarily the process that is wrong, it is the 'dressing up' of the process as something more than it actually is.

> *"A life is not important except in the impact it has on other lives"*
>
> Jackie Robinson

AI on the other hand allows for a form of co-creation which can genuinely involve stakeholders in the production of something from the ground up. And if that is what you want to do, AI is a great mechanism to do it. In this example, if it is done genuinely and properly, the very fact that stakeholders have been actively involved and the emergent ideas are taken on board is a successful outcome in itself.

Now let's go to the other end of the scale, let's drill down on that word outcome and follow it through to its inevitable end. When people talk about outcomes they are often what I will call 'interim' outcomes. In other words they are only a step on the outcome journey that should end at impact on the 'bottom line' of the business or service; this is usually either profits or impact (or both). When I make the distinction between profits OR impact, I should say that even in totally service oriented organisations (e.g. local government) there is a need to provide value for money – i.e. highest levels of effective service in the most cost effective manner.

So, even in cases where there is an interim outcome for the organisation (e.g. reduction in sickness rates amongst employees), we would expect to see a related increase in that bottom line at some point.

But now to the rub. Generally, the further down the line you travel in terms of measuring impact, the more tenuous the link between the intervention and the outcome.

At one end of the scale, evaluation sheets at the end of an AI intervention have a clear and undisputed link between perceptions of the quality of the work conducted and the results of the evaluation. However, this measure is a poor indicator of longer term impact on the bottom line. Just because people feel great at the end of a fun day does not naturally equate to improvement back at base.

At the other end of the scale, a rise in profits for the private sector organisation is actually all about the bottom line – however to link that tangibly with the AI intervention raises all sorts of questions. Those questions centre on the myriad of other factors that may have impacted on that result.

All this provides a real dilemma and we seem to have gone around in circles, or as my Aikido instructor used to say – 'it makes you think you don't know what to think'!

So where do we go with this? Is there value in seeking to measure the results of an AI (or any other) OD intervention? Let's quickly explore the options on this and the pros and cons.

> *"God and Nature first made us what we are, and then out of our own created genius we make ourselves what we want to be. Follow always that great law. Let the sky and God be our limit and Eternity our measurement"*
>
> *Marcus Garvey*

Option 1 – measure nothing. There is an attraction in this to somebody who has witnessed some organisations committing significant resources to measuring results - and where the benefit of this activity is unproven. Where the measurement of outcomes becomes an industry in itself to the detriment (by the allocation of resources away from doing the actual job) of the function of the organisation.

This scenario is an unlikely one in most organisations these days, although I am aware of some who do go down this route. The obvious downside of this strategy is that organisations can continue spending money on activities that have minimal benefit. Business development and improvement becomes a gamble that may or may not pay off. Some organisations get away with this for many years, but ultimately they will inevitably develop pockets of the organisation that are being 'carried' by other sections performing at high levels. This would be especially true in larger organisations.

Conclusion? Measure nothing, as attractive as this is in some ways, is not an option in my opinion.

Option 2 – measure everything. When I was in the Merchant Navy in my late teens I went around the world in a refrigerated cargo ship that also doubled as a cadet training facility. One of the sayings was 'if it moves salute it, if it doesn't paint it'. This was based on the fact that in order to keep 30 cadets busy on a one-month trip to New Zealand, most of our time was allocated to painting the ship. I wouldn't care to guess how many coats of paint those white railings and red decks had on them over the years.

> *"Its not (it ain't) what you do it's the way that you do it"*
>
> Song title by Melvin "Sy" Oliver and James "Trummy" Young

I am sure there are few organisations who have the luxury these days of trying to think of ways to fill employee's time, but there are those that become obsessive over impact measurement and KPIs (key performance indicators), trying to measure anything that moves! This is to some degree driven by regulation and inspection in some sectors, but within others it is just part of an OCD (obsessive, compulsive disorder) element within the organisation.

This activity would be worthwhile if it actually resulted in a proportionate improvement in the bottom line – i.e. if the improvements in service and/or profit were significantly greater than the resources required to conduct the analysis of KPIs. It would also be worthwhile if the mechanisms used to measure the KPIs were robust, relevant and accurate – i.e. if the right things were being measured in the right way in order to get the right results.

The interesting thing here is that within these OCD organisations, if the quality performance team are producing statistics that indicate the organisation or team are performing badly, the blame (and it is that, however you dress it up) generally gets landed on the people doing the job. There is rarely consideration of the possibility that it is actually the work of the quality performance team and how they carry out their role that is a contributory factor in this!

It is at this point that I should 'throw in' another important element to this debate (even if the debate is with myself). You may remember that one of the assumptions of AI is that 'the act of asking questions of an organisation, or group, or individual influences them in some way'. It might not surprise you to know that I actually believe this. And if this is true, how any research or evaluation is carried out into performance levels and what is done with this data is critically important. In terms of research methodologies, there is an acceptance within some strands (e.g. Action Research) that the researcher cannot be the invisible fly on the wall, going unnoticed and having no impact on the subject of the research. In fact there is acknowledgement that not only does the researcher have an impact on the subject, but he/she subtly changes the actual results of the research.

> *"Facts are stubborn, but statistics are more pliable"*
>
> *Mark Twain*

In AI thinking, if the focus of any questioning is on the problems or deficits within the organisation, this can actually affect the subjects (usually workforce) in a negative manner. Conversely, if the focus is on what is working, this has a positive effect. This is an oversimplification but demonstrates the point.

Conclusion? The scatter gun, let's measure everything approach to quality measurement is not ideal. It potentially takes resources away from the front line, it can be crude in its operation and conclusions, and it can become a factor mitigating against improved performance.

Option 3 – dare I call it – the middle way. This option calls for an honest, considered and proportionate approach to measuring the success of any intervention. In this case an AI intervention.

As stated earlier, the first and pretty obvious step is to be clear about what you want from the intervention. This is actually a critical part of the AI process (the Define Stage) regardless of whether you intend to measure it or not. This can range from lower scale interim outcomes, through to bottom-line impact. The important thing here is to be clear and honest with yourself and the people involved. Don't dress it up as something it isn't and don't be tokenistic.

These desirable outcomes can be driven by a management agenda or come from employees and other stakeholders. Ideally they should cover all these people's views and ideas about what areas (topics) need to be focused on. In reality, management usually leads the way on this (i.e. it is they who initiate the AI process) but other stakeholders can then contribute to the debate. One way stakeholders can contribute is through that very simple 'three wishes' question.

Secondly, if possible, embed aspects of the desired outcomes into the wording of the Discovery and Dream questions. If one of the desired outcomes was the earlier example of reduced sickness levels, this would be woven into the Discovery Stage by asking people to reflect on examples of low sickness levels and why this had occurred. It could also be reflected in the Dream Stage by asking staff to visualise a future where sickness levels were extremely low; and to describe what would be happening to facilitate this.

Next, during the Design and Delivery stages, again start to bring back the focus to the intended outcomes. Don't let this rule out issues that do not match these predetermined areas of focus, these should have equal validity, but don't lose focus on these initial outcome statements.

Lastly, firm up your outcome measures and how you are going to assess and monitor these. All the outcome measures will not be apparent until the end of the Design Stage, and actually, if AI is embedded into the organisation's way of working, may extend beyond this. Who is going to take responsibility for this is another question. Do you want to engage the participants in deciding this and being part of the monitoring process or not?

You could decide to have a discreet independent group carrying out this function, but then would you want or need to feed back the results to participant groups?

This then leads on to conversations about potential strategies to monitor and measure the outcomes, if you want to do this. If all you wanted from the exercise were high levels of involvement, feedback and ideas in relation to your area of focus, and high levels of satisfaction at the end of the process, this is relatively easy to measure. And in terms of timescales these can all be measured during, or at the end of the process.

Taking our other example, if you wanted to reduce levels of staff sickness, the measurement post course would be relatively simple. However, what would not be simple would be to attribute this solely to the AI intervention.

Conclusion? These are all questions that the AI fraternity tend not to discuss or agree on – i.e. some do not discuss it and some discuss it and disagree on its importance or relevance. My view is that this whole area is important and needs discussion and response. The broad areas laid out in option 3 are, for me, desirable in most cases, and some degree of impact assessment should be planned for and delivered.

Why do I say this? Because doing nothing misses opportunities. Not attempting to measure impact misses opportunities to improve and refine the process (based on outcome) and it misses opportunities to confirm and celebrate what really matters (impact). Alternatively, attempting to measure everything that moves has the potential to wrap the whole process in a 'blanket' of analysis that could ultimate dull the whole creative, spontaneous aspect of AI – the thing that makes it shine.

# 8. HOW CAN AI BE APPLIED

AI can be used in a whole range of ways, in fact the more you use it and understand it the more applications you will discover. This applies to organisations, groups and individuals. But the principles remain the same – what are we doing well and why, where do we want to be in the future, how are we going to get there, and how are we going to deliver? People engage fully with the process, both on an individual and group level. Engagement generates ownership and ownership generates action. The application of AI on an ongoing basis can result in generative change – change that is sustainable and has a life of its own.

So here are five broad ways AI can be used – consultation, self evaluation, culture change, thematic reviews and personal development. The section following this will then look in more detail at more specific case studies and scenarios.

### 1. Consultation

One of the features of AI is the high levels of engagement with as wide a range of stakeholders as possible. This is not just tokenistic consultation, but real involvement (co-production) in key elements of change (whatever that might be).

If you are organising an event that seeks to truly engage stakeholders, the AI process is a great way to do it. And if your gauge of success is only the number of people involved, the amount of new ideas generated (and integrated into any resultant programme), and levels of satisfaction at the end of the event – that is fine.

## 2. Self evaluation

Many organisations within the care and education sectors are expected (or required) to have an ongoing process of self evaluation. As a result of this they then have to prepare a service improvement or business plan. A familiar part of this process, particularly within education, is the identification of strengths and weaknesses. Interestingly the terminology (in Wales) has changed over recent years from shortcomings to 'areas for improvement'. Whether the positive psychology movement or AI has influenced this I doubt, but it is interesting.

In terms of a definition of success in relation to self evaluation, one of the main criteria would be how accurately the organisation has identified both its strengths and areas for improvement. This is on the basis that if it does this honestly and accurately there is more likelihood that areas for development will get addressed. There is also a strong emphasis on engaging key stakeholders with this process (inspectors will often ask members of the workforce and learners if they have been involved).

*"To ensure continuous improvement in standards of education and training, all providers need to ensure that self-evaluation and self-assessment are a regular part of their work"*

*Estyn (Wales Education and Training Inspectorate)*

As with consultation, one of the critical elements here is engaging with key stakeholders – i.e. this in itself is a definition of success. Over and above this, however, there is an obvious expectation that through this engagement accurate judgements emerge on performance and a resultant action plan is implemented. At a later stage, of course, these actions should result in measurable outcomes; in relation to education this usually equates to numbers and levels of qualifications.

## 3. Culture change

Cultures develop in all organisations. They are not planned for and they are often not recognised until behaviours arise that are noticeable for some reason. These behaviours can end up being beneficial for the organisation in terms of reputation and performance, or destructive in terms of both.

This whole area has been particularly noticeable within financial services over recent years. We are currently (2012) experiencing a wave of instances where individuals within organisations have caused immense damage through their inappropriate actions. In many cases these actions have been the result of particular cultures that have developed within some organisations that are characterised by behaviours that are often defined as unethical. These behaviours will generally not be down to the random activities of a few people, but more likely indicative of a wider systemic culture within the organisation, or parts of it.

Changing these behaviours can be incredibly difficult and certainly it is my strongly held belief that traditional methods of trying to challenge these behaviours directly through training is doomed to failure in many cases. This is because the behaviours are the consequence of many years of informal interactions and communications that have resulted in this shared way of looking at the world. This becomes a little bit like a 'micro climate', a condition that is particular, in this case, to a group rather than a geographical location. Essentially this IS Social Constructionism in action, in this case it is a 'destructive' example.

> *"Creative thinking is not a talent, it is a skill that can be learnt. It empowers people by adding strength to their natural abilities which improves teamwork, productivity and where appropriate profits"*
>
> Edward de Bono

These cultures develop (and spread) over a period of time and are the result of tens of thousands of 'micro moments'. Informal communications that take place within groups that slowly get accepted as the norm. These types of behaviours will not be remedied by relatively short term training interventions, what needs to occur is that new conversations need to take place that centre on a future that the organisation deems is more appropriate (in this case ethical).

AI is a way to do this. Not as a one off exercise, but by embedding AI thinking into the organisation based around desirable themes and topics. Discovering and sharing the experiences of those people who are acting in synergy with the desired future (and they will be there) and building on this towards the future vision.

### 4. Thematic approaches

Examples of thematic approaches are almost endless. They can range from behavioural issues within an organisation through to highly technical. Let me give you an example of both of these.

Many organisations deliver equality and diversity training, either because they think this is the correct thing to do or because of legislation (or both). Organisations traditionally respond to this in familiar ways, providing training that seeks to identify and improve 'bad' behaviour in relation to attitudes connected to race, gender etc.

AI can turn this on its head, engaging people in a process of identifying positive examples of respect and valuing based on their own experiences. This is then used as the foundation for moving the organisation towards that vision of genuine 'unconditional positive regard' (to use Carl Rogers' phrase) towards all others – the essence of truly valuing all people regardless of what or who they are. This process is not based on 'preaching' to people and telling them how they should behave, but starts from exploring their own experiences of being valued and what that means to them.

Going to the other end of the scale, AI can be applied to highly technical issues. Take the classic example of the database that has just been purchased at great expense and users are tearing their hair out trying to make it work for them in their day-to-day roles.

This will almost certainly be the result of poor planning and implementation involving people on the one side (the client) who has all the job specific knowledge and the supplier who has all the technical knowledge. The result is a system that has all the required functionality (it does the things it is supposed to do) but takes little account of how it needs to respond to the needs of the users (basically the user interface).

> *"The organisations of the future will increasingly depend on the creativity of their members to survive. Great Groups offer a new model in which the leader is an equal among Titans. In a truly creative collaboration, work is pleasure, and the only rules and procedures are those that advance the common cause"*
>
> Warren Bennis

The traditional response to this is to identify the problems with the system and seek to fix them. The issue with this is that classically, if you ask the techies they will say the users are at fault and if you ask the users they will say it's the system. Of course in reality it is never that straightforward and there will be aspects of both that will be problematic.

Ideally everyone needs to be in the same room to address this, but if the focus is directly on the problems, blame and recrimination (and possibly bloodshed) will surely ensue!

Using an AI approach gets over this. It creates a conducive environment that takes its starting point from examples of what is working (and they will be there) then moves on to a solution focus. Problems are resolved but within a positive framework.

### 5. Personal development

These are just two examples of the hundreds out there that may be pertinent to your organisation.

Many people just use AI in relation to working with individuals. Again I will provide two examples.

The classic application is in relation to one-to-ones, supervision, coaching type scenarios. Situations where you are trying to support an individual rather than a group in journeying from A to B. By now I am sure I almost do not need to spell this out... we start engaging the person in conversations about what is working in their life (in this case their work life) and why. This can be an open conversation or centred on identified themes. It can be, and is, a substantial conversation, particularly the discovery of the contributory factors (the why). This starting point is engaging and empowering for the individual, but also provides them with something real to take out into their wider role. Something that will assist them to develop and improve.

> *"Person Centred Planning discovers and acts on what is important to a person. It is a process for continual listening and learning, focussing on what is important to someone now and in the future, and acting on this in alliance with their family and their friends"*
>
> *Thompson J. Kilbane J. Sanderson H*

The second part of the conversation focuses on a desired future, again this can be open or centred on key themes. As with the organisational application, blue sky thinking should be encouraged on the basis that the Design Stage will bring it back to earth (whilst also giving ideas the 'wings to fly').

Finally, actions are agreed and the process continues over time to ensure follow through and sustainability.

The second example is related to Person Centred Planning (PCP). This is a process that is fairly unique to the care sector and enables people who are receiving support (e.g. social or health care) to have a meaningful input into their plan of care.

Traditionally this plan was, and still mainly is, driven by the agendas of professionals (social workers, health workers, specialists) and is nearly always biased towards what the person can't do – i.e. their needs and deficits.

Person centred planning involves two stages, firstly creating a picture (profile) of the person based on their own perspective - what they can do, are interested in, can give etc. Then creating a plan to deliver on this.

The AI process can be effectively used to help create that profile based on discovering activities and experiences they enjoy and why. Again this can be open or thematic (e.g. looking at a particular lesson in school that a young person enjoyed, within an overall scenario of lack of engagement within education). This is then supplemented by 'dreaming' about the ideal future – an activity that is already part of the PCP process.

In relation to 'dreaming' within PCP, there are always a range of views about how realistic this process should be, just like with AI. My view is that even if the young girl with multiple disabilities wants to be an airline pilot that is OK. Why is it OK? It's OK because the next question is 'what is it about being an airline pilot that appeals to you'? What comes from that question is valuable information that might result in her first holiday abroad on a plane, or just trips to the local airport. If the original dream had been dismissed, none of this would have been discovered.

I should add that I have used this application of AI quite recently when I was providing PCP training to a series of children's homes within North Wales. Interestingly, there are few examples of the use of PCP within residential services to young people across the UK. In fact, when I did a web search I found none. Children's services often profess to be 'child centred', but then on analysis the process that drives the support to the child, the Placement Plan, is heavily weighted by professional assessment and a focus on needs and deficits.

Within this project, I worked with the provider to deliver training that resulted in profiles (think assessments) being developed by the young person, based on their strengths and interests. The teams then used this profile to enter into a dialogue with each young person about their desired future. Finally actions were agreed that then fed into the Placement Planning process. The result? Young people having some level of 'ownership' of their Placement Plans and, in theory, some level of engagement and ownership of the strategies required to move them forward in a positive manner. This is also an example of co-creation; moving beyond consultation (what do you think about what we think) to true participation.

On a final note, within this piece of work we had those same questions raised about how much we 'allow' young people to dream the dream. The two actual examples given to me were, 'what do we do when X says I want to be a drug dealer – or a prostitute?'. For those not familiar with children in care – very sadly these can be the aspirations of some young people. The answer was the same as the airline pilot above. Don't dismiss it. Don't patronise and say 'OK, fine, we will write that down in your plan'. Enter into a dialogue about 'what is it about being a drug dealer that appeals to you?'. What came out when we explored this with the staff teams, based on conversations they had had with young people, were things like – to be respected, flexible hours, power, being part of something, money, etc. Now here are a set of aspirations we CAN work with!

# 9. FIVE SCENARIOS

To follow on from the last section let me offer you five very different organisational scenarios and case studies in terms of the application of AI. These include situations I have had first hand experience of and ones that many of you will be able to relate to. I have made reference to some of them elsewhere in this book but let's explore them in a little bit more detail.

I am very aware that I have rushed and condensed the AI process here, this is on the basis that it is explained fully earlier in the book. What I want to do is put this into context within a scenario. And the only thing that makes these scenarios any different is usually the nature of the questions and who is involved in the process.

### Scenario 1 – customer feedback

Most organisations have some form of mechanism to determine the views of their customers. This is either done in an ad-hoc and unstructured way (i.e. let's just chat to people when we get the chance) or as part of a formalised programme of ongoing evaluation. In the case of the formal process, comparisons are usually made over time to determine if satisfaction levels are rising or falling. Also, dependant on the breadth of questions asked, there may be a more sophisticated analysis of different elements of the organisation in order to target responses.

Whatever the process used, what is common is that the focus is on those customers who made critical comments – i.e. who identified problems and concerns in relation to a product or service they received. That is not to say that positive comments are ignored, they may be used as part of PR campaigns or in some cases (rare) captured as case studies for use within staff training. However, the point is that the main focus of activity is on analysing what went wrong and how to remedy it.

> *"A cardinal principle of Total Quality escapes too many managers: you cannot continuously improve interdependent systems and processes until you progressively perfect interdependent, interpersonal relationships"*
>
> Stephen Covey

Now… let me say again, in my view there is nothing wrong with seeking to fix the problems, although some others in the AI world might disagree with me. This is particularly so when those problems are having an immediate and detrimental impact on the customer. For example, if a customer was promised a service or product by a particular date and they have not received it, that needs to be addressed as quickly as possible. Also, if as part of the 'investigation', you discover that a member of staff who caused the problem has a history in relation to this – this needs dealing with and addressing, including the capability route if necessary.

HOWEVER, and this is the key point in this and other scenarios – focusing on problems is not the best way to respond to deeper rooted systemic issues of business improvement, in this case, specifically related to customer service.

So what would we do? Of course, if this was a workshop or presentation I would just stand in front of you and ask you that question! But its not, it's a book, and I am hoping you are thinking the obvious – yes - we carry out an AI exercise!

This will start by deciding if you have the capability in-house to facilitate the AI process. If you have learned to ride the 'AI bike' the answer may be yes. If you have not, I would suggest the answer is no. And of course there are a range of options here, you might feel more confident and it might be more appropriate, to apply aspects of AI thinking rather than a 'full blown' AI exercise. These 'aspects' could include drilling down on positive responses and possibly inviting these customers (the ones who responded positively) to attend some focus groups. These groups could incorporate Discovery questions that seek to explore what contributed to the positive customer experience.

The upside of this limited approach is that you could possibly do this without external facilitation and the resources (internal and external) that this would demand. The downside is that the impact of such an exercise could be limited – i.e. it would only be you, or you and a few colleagues, that would be experiencing the feedback directly. This reduces opportunities for ownership and buy-in from those people who may need to be shifted in relation to their thinking and behaviour.

So let's say we decide to instigate a full AI exercise, either facilitated externally or internally. A planning group would be formed and all the areas raised in the earlier chapter (The application of AI – the 5D cycle – Define) would be considered. Conversations could include:

- Reflection on purpose and mission of the organisation (which will inevitably have some reference to the customer in most cases);
- The areas of focus – the topics;
- Who is involved – the stakeholders internal and external. Management and front line workers;
- Logistics including options for a Summit and/or cascade approach;
- Desired outcomes and if any evaluation will take place of impact;
- Communication – how is it communicated to participants;
- Launch – will there be one;

One of the key decisions will be about topic choice. At one level this is clear – it is about customer satisfaction. At another, it may need to be more sophisticated, what aspect of customer satisfaction requires improvement? For example, if there are issues about the front-end call handling (e.g. reception), a question may need to be framed around this.

How this is phrased needs to take into consideration the people involved in the AI process. You will have decided to involve management and staff directly and indirectly involved in call handling. Ideally, you will also have decided to involve a number of customers. This may very well be the first time you have attempted to involve customers alongside staff in this type of environment (i.e. training, development, organisational development) but remember that using an AI framework makes this possible on the basis that it does not explicitly expose your shortcomings.

If you have managed to get this range of people involved you may want to phrase a Discovery question something like this – *'think back to a time when you experienced or witnessed exceptional customer service on the telephone. What contributed to that, what made it such a positive experience for you'?*

You will note that the way the question is worded focuses on a telephone experience in this case. It also allows for people to refer to experiences they have witnessed as well as those they have been directly involved in. This means that managers can comment on what they have witnessed and front-line staff can choose to comment on the work of their colleagues. Subtle changes in wording like this can make all the difference in relation to the AI process and how well it works. This is one reason why the Define Stage is so important.

You may decide to limit the exercise to that one topic; don't think that will result in limited feedback. What you will actually find is that the range of 'material' that gets shared will be significant as the process moves through the last 4Ds. However, you may also wish to explore other topics that are related, this could include issues such as IT (e.g. the Customer Management System).

A question will also need to be framed in relation to the Dream Stage. This could be something like – *'imagine we are one year in the future and we have just won a UK award for excellence in responding to customer enquiries. What would that look like? What would be happening within the organisation and how would people be behaving?*

Again you will notice that this question makes specific reference to 'what would that look like?'. It is really important to encourage and enable people to think visually as well as in theoretical terms. There is also a 'steer' for people to consider behaviours. This might not be necessary but it gives an example of how the use of targeted words can be used to frame the focus of the inquiry. And don't forget, these questions need to be informed by as wide a range of stakeholders as possible. This will inevitably be driven in the first instance by management in most cases, but the 'three wishes' question can be put out to potential participants prior to the process in order to explore where they see potential improvement and development.

Once all the above has been agreed as part of the Define Stage the rest becomes relatively straightforward – i.e. as with any project management activity the most important part is the planning.

Firstly the Discovery Stage will be rolled out. This will either be as part of an extended summit/workshop activity or within groups or one to one. If it is incorporated within a workshop people will talk in pairs, themes will be identified and shared, and resultant examples of peak practice and contributory factors will be captured (generally on flip chart sheets) for use within the Design Stage.

The Dream Stage will then focus people's minds on the desired future for the organisation, based on the topic choice and pre-determined questions. People will work in groups (ideally mixed in terms of responsibilities, role and focus) and they will be encouraged to be creative with how they record their thoughts and ideas – i.e. they should be fun. Also (and this question nearly always arises), they should not limit their aspirations. This is on the basis that the use of Provocative Propositions and the Design Stage shapes those ideas within a framework of being grounded in reality.

Next the Provocative Propositions are introduced and the same groupings can often respond to these. This leads into Design where groups (that can change into role specific groupings) build on the best of what is already occurring (from Discovery) in order to deliver on the Dream. Lastly, the Delivery Stage focuses on issues of sustainability – how will we do what we said we were going to do… long after the mood we said it in has passed! And remember, based on research, the organisations that do this best embed AI thinking and working into their ongoing processes (e.g. meetings, supervision etc.).

## Scenario 2 – IT systems

This is the type of scenario that generally does not get associated with AI due to its seemingly highly technical nature. I have made mention of it earlier in the book but want to explore it in more detail.

At this point I should say that I actually have some background in IT that started with 'dabbles' on some of the first consumer computers. I still remember my old Amstrad 464 – can you imagine a cassette tape drive instead of a hard disc drive! However, my first 'proper' foray into the corporate world of IT started when I was working for an inspection unit within a Local Authority (that no longer exists) in North Wales. The Inspection Unit (inspecting care providers) had purchased a computer system at considerable cost. This system was designed to record information about providers and to track the RICE (Registration, Inspection, Complaints, Enforcement) process. It had been purchased from a high profile national IT company in England.

The scenario that followed was familiar. Like the seemingly endless examples you read about in the press involving failed IT systems, often costing millions of pounds. This system (which I hasten to add did not cost millions) did everything it was scoped to do – i.e. it had all the functionality required, but the users hated it! To be more precise the interface was extremely cumbersome, with users having to go through multiple screens to complete minor (often mandatory) tasks. The result? They did not use it properly, or when they did, it took so long to do that they fell behind on other work. Ultimately they slowly reverted back to other familiar systems such as spreadsheets.

This is a long story and I will not bore you with the detail, but it resulted in me designing an alternative system in a programme called Lotus Approach. Bear in mind I had no experience in either designing databases or using Lotus Approach. I should say that Lotus Approach was an IBM product that most database purists would frown on – but it did the job in this case. I then went on to sell this system to around 20 other Local Authorities throughout the UK.

The reason I was able to do this was firstly because I knew the job – I was an inspector who had to deliver on all the processes that the database was tracking. Secondly, I had developed the IT skills to conceptualise how this should and could be translated into a database. This is actually very unusual. Normally people either know the job or they know IT, and this is where the problems start. A classic case of 'lost in translation', the start of a developing dialogue that seeks to meet the needs of users but often only meets the needs (as defined in the specification) of the IT professionals.

And this is not the fault of those IT professionals, it is the fault (dare I say it) of the project managers who are managing this whole development process. This development process that is, in effect, a dialogue about 'where are we now', 'where do we want to get to', and 'how are we going to get there'. For it to work all these people need to have a series of conversations that lead to a solution that is fit for purpose. And how those conversations are framed needs to ensure that all the key stakeholders have their views and ideas valued. This may seem rather 'romantic' to some, but the consequences of not getting this right at the start are out there to see in the virtual scrapheap of trashed databases.

To emphasise my point. Firstly, computerised databases are often designed taking little regard (or involvement) of the end user. Secondly, when they are in place users often blame the designers and designers blame the users – same old same old.

Now let me come back to our scenario, which is actually based on a real-life case I used as part of AI training. This particular organisation wanted to up-skill some of their staff in AI and I arranged a four-day training workshop in response to this. To start I used a scenario based on the three wishes question to participants. This 'exposed' issues about their IT system but within a positive framework.

We then went on to agree the Discovery and Dream questions. These were as follows:

Discovery – *'Think about a time when you were using X and the system delivered most effectively in terms of its use. This could be related to inputting information into the system or extracting information / reports from the system. If you are able, explain how this may have ultimately benefitted the people being supported by the service. What contributed to this and how – people, environment, systems?'*

Dream – *'Imagine we are 12 months into the future and changes have been made to the X system. It is now being used in a consistent way by everyone and you are totally confident in its use and benefits. The result of this is a more efficient and effective service'.*

- *What would this look like and what would be happening (e.g. in terms of what people are doing, the way things are working etc)?*
- *Who is benefitting and how'?*

Of note is the fact that we had both users of the system and internal IT staff in the training. Internal IT were the people who had been involved in the commissioning of the system and who provided the current support to users.

The wording of both the questions was carefully phrased to bring in elements of concern (e.g. consistency and perceived benefit), but as you can see, using an AI approach provided a positive, non-adversarial framework.

The underlying tensions between the two groups of staff was apparent during the AI exercise (which bear in mind was being used for the purposes of training in this case) but it was positive that they completed the task without getting into the blame game.

The actions coming out of the exercise (i.e. out of Design and Delivery) were very relevant and would have resulted in an improvement in a problematic situation. However, because it was part of a training programme we did not have the involvement of managers who would ultimately endorse the rationale for the decisions and resultant spend. In this case the AI process succeeded as a training exercise, but failed in terms of impact.

So what were the lessons here for me?

Firstly, do not choose AI scenarios within training that are too real – i.e. that are high profile and actually need addressing as a matter of urgency. What this can do is create expectations that cannot be followed through.

Secondly, a reminder that the involvement of management is imperative in most situations on the basis that most decisions require management sign-off.

## Scenario 3 – HR processes

Human Resource Departments are the people who usually have to deal with the fall-out of breakdowns in communication within organisations. And breakdowns of communication are the most common cause of much more serious problems within organisations. HR departments are also the people (in my view) who have the most to benefit from embracing an AI approach for systemic issues.

The scenario I am going to share with you is not one where I used an AI intervention. However, it is real in the sense that I was directly involved as an external consultant.

It occurred a few years ago and involved me being asked to support the Chair of a disciplinary hearing following a complex external investigation. The reason that I was brought in was because the focus of one of the resultant disciplinary cases was a member of the HR team. On that basis it was considered not appropriate for HR to support the Chair in the hearing.

Ultimately there was found to be no case against the individual concerned from a disciplinary standpoint, however, there were (as is nearly always the case) a number of wider organisational learnings. These learnings centred, in this case, on how effectively and/or promptly management had responded to concerns about the behaviour of one member of staff.

The classic response to this from a systemic point of view (bear in mind the immediate 'problem' has now been dealt with in a traditional and appropriate way) is to review what went wrong and seek to fix it. The result of this would almost certainly lead to some teams and individuals regressing into corners of the 'ring'; blame and counter blame; politics etc.

The alternative approach would be to initiate an AI exercise – and again I can nearly hear you describing the process before I have even written it!

We would engage with managers and HR staff, at the very least, to explore the following questions (or similar). Ideally we might like to also involve a representative staff group, some of whom might have been subject to disciplinary processes and 'emerged' out of the other end unscathed and better people for it!

Discovery – *'think about a time when you experienced or witnessed a disciplinary process that resulted in a resolution of the situation and an ultimately positive outcome for all concerned. What happened, where were you, who was involved, what processes were used, how did people behave'?*

Dream – *'imagine we are 18 months into the future, the HR department has dealt with six high profile disciplinary cases, including one involving a member of their own staff. All these have been highly successful for all parties involved resulting in performance improvement. Describe what that would look like – what would people be doing and how would they be behaving, what processes and systems would be in place and what other things would we be seeing'?*

You will note that the above Discovery question focuses on impact. What we are doing here is allowing for a negative experience that was ultimately turned around. You may remember earlier I spoke about the choice between the focus on positive experience or positive outcome, or maybe both. They both have an important part to play and how they are used needs to be carefully considered given the scenario.

You will also notice that the Dream question makes specific reference to responding to a disciplinary issue within an HR team. This again shows how carefully constructed and 'intelligent' questions can make the AI process more targeted, relevant and ultimately successful.

> *"One of his greatest assets is optimism – that is, he sees a profitable outcome in practically every life situation, including disastrous ones. Years ago he spilled toxic pesticide into a cut on his hand and suffered permanent heart and liver damage from it. In his opinion it was all for the best because he was able to sell an article about his experience ("Would you Die for Your Plants") to a gardening journal"*
>
> The Orchid Thief

## Scenario 4 – the NHS

About nine months ago I read about a piece of work that was going to be tendered out in Wales, it read as follows:-

*'SPECIFICATION for a programme of awareness raising training to enable hospital based staff in Wales to better understand the needs of patients with learning disabilities'.*

It went on to say that:

*'In September 2011, the Public Service Ombudsman for Wales reported following the*

death of an individual with learning disabilities in Morriston Hospital in 2007. The Ombudsman made a number of recommendations including:

*"learning disability awareness training for staff and reminders for staff about appropriate care and relevant audits and inspections".*

*'The Minister for Health and Social Services met with the family of the deceased and agreed to secure a programme of awareness raising for hospital-based staff to ensure they are provided with an understanding of the particular needs of patients with a learning disability'.*

The aim of the piece of work was described as:

*'To develop and deliver activities to support an awareness campaign for health professionals and front line support staff to meet the recommendations set out in the Public Service Ombudsman for Wales report'*

The tender document went on to say that the 'campaign' should deliver 'at least three awareness raising sessions' within eight locations throughout Wales. It also described this activity as 'training'.

What has happened since then I do not know. Almost certainly awareness raising training will have been held and hopefully at least some individual staff within the NHS will have improved their understanding of the very specific needs of people with a learning disability (and others who may have limited understanding and communication).

Now let me bring you back to the present time. A friend and colleague of mine (we will call her Jan – not her real name) who has been awarded an MBE for her advocacy work with vulnerable people was visiting her friend in a local hospital. It so happened that this friend had a learning disability and was older. Her experience in one small snapshot within that hospital was not good.

I am not going to go into the detail here, but it included poor practice that endangered the life of Mary (not her real name) and highly questionable behaviours by a range of staff within the hospital. This included a doctor asking Jan (who told me the story) if she would sign a 'do not resuscitate' form for Mary whilst she was standing in front of Mary at her bedside! I should add that Mary is now out of hospital and was last seen doing her shopping in the local Sainsburys.

In contrast, a day later Jan went into the hospital again to visit Mary. She went to her bed and the curtains were closed. As she stood outside the curtain she heard a member of staff talking to Mary in a very sensitive and gentle manner. She could also see that this member of staff was holding Mary's hand.

As it turned out this member of staff was quite new to the nursing profession. Jan told her how wonderful she had been and thanked her for her kindness. This was especially pertinent given her previous experiences.

All these events led to Jan making a formal complaint to the hospital which, at this point, has not been processed. However, let's explore what the hospital could do in response.

One would hope (as we are all potential customers of the NHS) that there would be a 'classic' investigation and the people directly involved would be identified and remedial action taken. If the concerns were proven this may involve disciplinary action and/or some form of support and training. Inevitably, blame would be attributed to the people involved as part of this, but of course the wider dynamics in terms of cultural and systemic issues would remain unresolved.

It is at this point that we should acknowledge that the NHS within the UK is often referred to as a world leader in terms of quality and equality of access. I am somebody who believes that is true. However, the NHS is also a massive organisation, and the larger the organisation the slower it takes to 'turn'. Going back to my experiences as a teenager in the Merchant Navy, I remember my days as a Navigating Cadet. I was serving on board the M.V. Otaio, a large refrigerated cargo ship operated by P&O New Zealand Shipping Company. Apart from painting and saluting officers; now and again we got the opportunity to spend time steering the ship. Hell of a risk you might be thinking, putting a 16-year old in charge of steering a multi-million pound vessel! However, bear in mind we were in the middle of the Atlantic Ocean, where the worst thing we might hit was a flying fish (yes there is such a thing) or piece of drift wood.

One of your first thoughts when steering a ship weighing 13,314 gross tons is that the steering mechanism is broken. You turn the wheel and nothing happens, literally. So you turn it some more... then more. Then, something happens. The ship starts to turn, but to a much greater degree than you wanted. Bear in mind this could be happening a couple of minutes after you first turned the wheel. So you panic slightly. Not because you are going to hit anything but because you have been told to hold a course, indicated by the compass, and you are starting to veer off to a significant degree. What you then do is to repeat all of the above, but in the other direction. You turn the wheel back. Nothing happens. You turn it some more etc. What you end up with is a ship that is zig-zagging across the ocean. And the rule of thumb is, the larger the ship, the more likely this is to occur and the more intense the effect.

So it is with organisations. The larger it is the longer it takes to turn. But all those interventions will ultimately have an impact after time, but rather than taking minutes as at sea, they might take years, dependant on the size of the organisation.

Get those interventions right and you will turn the organisation back on course. Get it wrong, and you will turn the organisation even more off course and the responses required to get it back will take even longer. Here we have the classic challenge of changing deeply rooted cultures that have embedded themselves over years. And at the heart of these changes are human dynamics. How individuals attempt to deal with challenges. How they relate to each other at a human level. And even the smallest events have a potential impact, an effect on the direction of the ship.

So how do we respond to this NHS example from an AI perspective? Firstly, the matter does need investigation and a traditional problem focused response. The hospital cannot afford for similar events to reoccur and needs to put into place focused strategies that will minimise this possibility. However, this is short-term 'patch work', it does not deal with the deeper systemic issues. Actually, it probably does not deal with the specific issues related to those members of staff either. Why? Because almost certainly other people will have 'had words' with them in the past and they will have been on other training courses that told them how they should behave. It either just went straight over their heads (think jigsaw pieces) or they were of the opinion that they knew better.

Once the immediate problems have been resolved to some degree, it is now possible to apply an AI approach to the more deeply rooted issues. One that does not repeat the same cycle of focusing on the problems and seeking to fix them.

The Define Stage would cover all the logistical issues outlined in other sections of this book and in the first scenario. In particular it would consider who to involve and what questions to ask - i.e. based on the topic choice.

Involvement would ideally need to include a range of staff, including specialisms and 'levels', together with other stakeholders – most obviously patients. This element would almost certainly make the AI intervention much more valuable than previous responses, just on the basis that management and customers would be involved. And why wouldn't they have been involved before... beyond people simply not being creative? Because - who wants to hang out their 'dirty laundry' in front of their primary customers! Again – the advantage of taking an AI approach is that the focus is on discovering what is working and why, together with aspirations for the future. Name, blame and shame is avoided, whilst still addressing the problematic issues through the Dream Stage.

So what question could you start with for the Discovery Stage, given the scenario above? How about the following...

*'Describe a time when you were involved in providing or receiving support within a hospital ward that was highly responsive to the needs of the patient and resulted in people feeling respected and valued'.*

What that simple little question does is as follows. Firstly it allows providers (NHS staff) and customers (patients) to identify with the question and respond to it in relation to their own experience. The only people who might struggle are managers who are remote to the front line, but hopefully they will have experienced this at some time in their past.

Secondly it focuses on impact – the service was responsive to people's needs.

Thirdly it allows people to share what is working and why, within an organisation that probably spends most of its time investigating what went wrong and why. It is liberating and it is refreshing. I know by now this is something that you will understand as an intrinsic part of the Discovery process. But I want to again stress how important this is, particularly when related to an organisation as big and complex as the NHS. And particularly when there will be a multitude of good practice examples to draw upon.

Lastly it draws out the critical factors (which a few people working in the health care sector just keep seeming to miss) of valuing people and treating them with respect. Something that actually costs nothing!

It is often very difficult to know how much to 'seed' questions and direct people a particular way. In this case it would have been an option not to mention 'valuing' and 'respect' in the hope that these would naturally emerge over the course of all the feedback. However, in this case these two areas are so critical that it is worth focusing participants' attention on them. What we then hope is that other critical areas emerge from the shared stories that talk about the importance of listening to the patient and how you do this when people have limited communication.

Of course you could address all of these issues (i.e. valuing, respect, listening etc.) through traditional training, and sadly the fact is that staff will have received this – but did it make any difference in these cases!?

The next stage is to engage participants in the Dream – *'imagine our hospital has just won a national award for patient care, this includes testimonials for the effectiveness of the care provided and of the way people are valued as individuals, what would that look like, what would be happening'?*

You can see the focus here on both clinical care and a person centred way of working, these being the two most important elements of the service. Participants may 'paint a picture' that includes higher levels of resources, but inevitably messages would emerge about the simple things that can be done in terms of the way people behave, communication, relationships etc.

The Design Stage would then involve people in agreeing actions that would deliver on the dream, bearing in mind the good practice that emerged from the Discovery exercise. Again, the use of Provocative Propositions would seek to balance and reconcile the tensions between what might be seen as unrealistic aspirations and a 'grounded' view of what is possible. Out of this would emerge creative ideas that would improve the service, both from a management perspective and 'exploiting' the knowledge of the front-line staff.

Participants would take ownership of actions to a far higher degree than compared to traditional training or awareness raising exercises. And if the AI way of thinking and working was embedded into the organisation, this would ensure that the self motivating and generative aspects of AI would really take hold.

### Scenario 5 – community engagement
About two years ago I was involved in supporting an initiative with an organisation based in Liverpool called 'Appreciating People'. The UK government had launched an initiative to identify communities in England that were experiencing high levels of anti-social behaviour (ASB). The government wanted to involve the local communities themselves in decisions about how to respond, on the basis that a blanket response did

not take into account the unique circumstances of each area.

This was a creative and innovative programme and was supported by hard cash. Each small community area would receive £10,000 to spend as they wished, on the basis that they engaged in a planning process. Our role was to facilitate the conversations about possible strategies that could be funded through this money. We involved as wide a range of stakeholders as possible, this included local residents, government and voluntary agencies, and the police.

A traditional approach would have centred on identifying what the problematic issues were and then to agree response strategies. Those conversations would have included stories of traumatic events that significantly impacted on residents' quality of life. They would have also inevitably led to suggestions of blame. Young people being blamed for their behaviours. The police being blamed for lack of response. We turned this around by taking an AI approach. This started by agreeing the intended aims of the workshop. Examples included:

- An increased understanding of ASB and resident confidence to be more knowledgeable and active in tackling ASB issues.

- The creation of common ground and more effective relationships at a local level between stakeholders to tackle ASB and to create a good neighbourhood for all ages.

- Creation and development of an action plan to spend the local £10,000 grant on local projects endorsed and recommended by local people.

- Creation of a user friendly action plan, which can be circulated to local people.

We then engaged people talking about (in pairs) what was working in their community based on the following question:

*'Think about a time when you have worked together with others (or seen others working together) to make a positive difference to the community. What was happening at the time, where were you, who was involved (not names), what prompted the action, what was the key thing that made a difference?*

This was a simple question that went to the core of what is important within communities, collaborative working between everyone to make a positive difference. The responses from this then started to provide an image of the positive core of that community.

The dream question was then introduced and people worked in groups to create their vision of how the local community could and would look. This was an opportunity to address things that were wrong, and to develop new and creative ideas. All within a positive framework that avoided recrimination and blame.

*'We are meeting again in 12 months – we have created a good neighbourhood for all, and have reduced ASB activity to a low level. Imagine what it would be like in detail. Describe what it might look like, what are young people doing, what are people doing / feeling? Describe what we have achieved, our successes and the challenges we have overcome'.*

In retrospect this question could have been more powerful and 'vibrant', possibly using that very word to emphasise the future image – i.e. 'we have created a vibrant and caring neighbourhood for all, rather than using the word 'good. This demonstrates the importance of how words are used to impact on the psychology of the group, the more powerful and descriptive the words the better, bearing in mind the group you are working with.

In terms of success, the project clearly ticked all but one box in the list of four above, plus more. The only objective that remained unknown (by me) was an aspect of number 2 – 'to create a good neighbourhood for all ages'. This is a classic example of an outcome that impacts 'on the bottom line' – what is really important. This is not to say this did not occur, just that my involvement ended before any evaluation of this.

### Wrapping up

So there we have five scenarios that I hope will give you a practical idea of how AI can be applied in five contrasting situations. I could literally write another book on extending these to almost any situation you could name. It really is the case that the more you grasp the thinking behind AI, the more potential you see for its application.

So now you know all about AI, or at least you're on the start of the journey of discovery, you might now be asking what do I do next?

*I keep wanting to go back to that analogy of fishing for facts. I can just see someone asking with great frustration, 'Yes, but which facts do you fish for? There's got to be more to it than that.' But the answer is that if you know which facts you're fishing for you're no longer fishing.*

Robert M Pirsig – Zen and the Art of Motorcycle Maintenance

# 10. WHAT NEXT?

Once you have finished reading this book the inevitable question arises, what next? Let's assume it has sown some seeds or inspired you in some way. It may even have provided just the piece of your jigsaw you were looking for and become the catalyst for the start of your AI journey – just like me many years ago.

At a personal level you may wish to read more literature on the subject. Books similar to this one and papers like those of Gervase Bushe. There are many out there and they all contain gems of personal discovery based on that Author's own journey. I certainly did this, and slowly built up my understanding of the thinking, principles, assumptions and methodology.

Of course reading books is never good enough. Let's take the analogy of riding a bicycle and let's pretend we are biking virgins.

Firstly, we could read a book on how to ride bikes from the best bike riders out there, experts who had refined bike riding to an art. Would it result in us being able to ride?

Next, we could go on a training course in a classroom being led by these same expert bike riders. Maybe they had even trained as teachers and were using the latest classroom techniques. They would tell us about their experiences, show us videos, tell us about the mechanics of balance and propulsion. Would that result in us being able to ride a bike?

Or, what about if we went on a practical training course and part of that course involved us getting on a bike and having a go? Alternatively, if we were really adventurous, we could just get on a bike without any training or help, keep falling off, but then slowly improve. Would that result in us being able to ride a bike?

Well I hope you said yes (even a reserved yes) to the last two scenarios. Because even if you fell off the bike a few times (with or without guidance) I think we would agree that 99% of us would end up being able to ride the bike. So it is with AI.

I actually did all these things. I was inspired by that chance comment by someone about their AI experience and went on my steep learning curve almost immediately. I read a book. Read another book. Tried incorporating elements of AI into aspects of my work (training, organisational reviews). Made mistakes. Had successes. Attended a residential course on AI. Moved forwards with a bit more confidence in terms of introducing and using the process. Went on another residential training course. And so on.

At the time of writing this book I have become a reasonably sized fish in a smallish pond. If you do a Google search on 'Wales Appreciative Inquiry' up pops Taith (my company) at number one, or at least it did in 2012! I am also asked to give talks at National events, deliver training in AI or to facilitate the process within organisations. As stated earlier in this book, it has totally changed the way I do my work, even when that work has no explicit connection to AI.

So let me explore a few scenarios in terms of your current position and what your options might be on your AI journey.

### I just want to read more

The first port of call for information on the subject has to be that amazing resource – t'internet (excuse the colloquialism). Probably the best source of information on the web is the Appreciative Inquiry Commons site. This states, '*a worldwide portal devoted to the fullest sharing of academic resources and practical tools on AI and the rapidly growing discipline of positive change. This site is a resource for you and many of us - leaders of change, scholars, students, and business managers - and it is proudly hosted by Case Western Reserve University's Weatherhead School of Management*'. The site includes descriptions of the process, case studies and much more, well worth a visit.

There are also a wide range of other books out there for further reading, a few of which have been listed at the end of this book.

What next?

## I want to use AI within my organisation

You may just read this book and think, we could really use this within our organisation. To do this you need to find a consultant who has experience and has some good testimonials behind them. Part of this will depend on where you live but from my experience there are good consultants in most countries.

You may be tempted to facilitate the process yourself, based on your newly acquired knowledge, but unless you have had training, or are experienced in the process I would not recommend this. I know of a number of stories of people who have picked up a little knowledge and then proudly proclaimed they were going to use the process to deliver some aspect of change or improvement. The result has often been unsuccessful. Worse than that, people who have been involved have had a distorted view of the AI process and it has actually proven to be counterproductive in a number of ways.

However… I am not going to totally rule out self-teaching (as many others might). In my view there is some merit in self-teaching in the early stages of the learning process, especially when this can be done by 'stealth'!

The stealth method has to be introduced slowly and quietly; under the radar. It works if you have natural abilities and experience in relation to facilitating groups and where you have truly been bitten by the AI bug, totally identifying with this way of thinking. You will start seeing opportunities to apply elements of AI, not necessarily as a whole 5D process but as distinct responses to specific business challenges.

For example, using the case from earlier in the book, you receive the results of your latest customer survey; then, rather than focusing on the 10% who rated you badly, you decide to focus on the 10% who thought you were exceptional. Not only do you look at what they said in their responses, but you get together a sample focus group to drill down on those contributory factors in order to spread the good practice more widely.

Then it comes to the annual review of the business plan by the senior management group. You decide that this would benefit from wider input and replicate the Dream Stage of AI with a much wider stakeholder group.

The point is, the more you think about AI and understand the principles behind it, the more you see opportunities to apply this in a creative way. Actually, this is where the true power of AI lies, in its ability to change the way you think about the world around you and the assumptions you had about this world – this is the transformative aspect.

## I want to teach others about AI

People who specialise in AI like myself usually go down one of two paths, they focus on training people in the principles and practice, or they facilitate the process in a consultancy type role.

I spoke above about facilitating the process, now let's look at training people in AI. The first thing to say is that to do this you really need to have the proverbial T shirt. The people with the smartest T shirts tend to be those who have practised the process the longest. They have been there and done it. Having said that, some of these people may not have the ability to train others on the basis that facilitating a process is different to training people in the process.

So, the obvious thing to state here is that offering training to others in AI comes after facilitating the process yourself, you really have to do one before the other. Apart from learning from your own implementation, you will also pick up 'tricks' from attending other people's training courses. As these two sources of learning grow and develop, so your expertise and confidence will grow. You then might get to a stage when you feel confident enough to train others.

At this point I should mention the words accreditation and qualifications. A lot of training 'out there' does not currently (as of 2012) offer this, however, there are a growing number of organisations and trainers who are developing this. Coming from the education world, and having been an HMI (Her Majesty's Inspector of education), I am of two views on this. Whilst accreditation is in theory an indication of quality (e.g. through external moderation etc.), it has also been abused in other sectors. Education has become such a competitive industry, that education providers are under more and more pressure to get results. And, because results equate to learner success, there is a worrying amount (in my view) of what could be called manipulation of the system to allow as many people as possible to succeed. What this results in is a denigration of the very thing that was supposed to provide a mark of quality – the accredited qualification.

Excuse me for the slightly tangential rant, but you get the point, whilst points might make prizes, accredited qualifications don't always make quality!

The best way to identify a good AI training course is, like with most things, through recommendation – accredited or not. The other factor, like with a restaurant, is to ensure that there is a consistency in terms of the tutors (or chef!).

**Training or facilitation**

If you start to practice AI, and get positive feedback, you will start to get asked to train others – it will happen. On the other side of the coin, as outlined above, you will see opportunities to use AI as a facilitation process. Increasingly I have lost the distinction between the two – i.e. the two are not mutually exclusive. In fact in most cases, each reinforces the other.

The best approach for me in relation to AI facilitation is to incorporate training as part of the process. The best approach for me in relation to AI training is to incorporate facilitation as part of the process.

What this results in is a situation whereby AI is used to facilitate change and improvement whilst at the same time core people within the organisation are up-skilled. The result of this is that the organisation is then not reliant on an outside consultant to maintain the required internal momentum and sustainability.

In conclusion, in my view any good abstract artist has a solid grounding in representational art (i.e. where you look at something and know what the hell it is – or even better, you look at it and it also talks to your heart as well as your head).

It is similar with martial arts like Aikido. Although many people think you have arrived when you get your black belt, actually you have just started. You have got a thorough grounding in the 'representational' aspects of all the moves, taught through many years of repetitive practice. But this is essential in order to form the basis of your development as an aikidōka (Aikido practitioner), moving onto more spontaneous responses to that unplanned and random attack that is coming your way. In fact in the real world (wherever that is!) somebody who is trained in Aikido would probably not use any of the formal techniques they practiced over those many years on the mat. They would just respond in a very natural and flowing way in order to neutralise the attack, maybe just using elements of those formal techniques.

And as it is with Zen. Life has to be firstly seen as distinctly 'this' or 'that' in order to see that actually there is something beyond, something far more subtle and non linear. As Pirsig shared in Zen and the Art of Motorcycle maintenance, something beyond just classical or romantic views of the world.

And so it is with AI. The AI practitioner has to paint by numbers first, earn his or her black belt, see what does work and what doesn't work as distinctly different in order to start appreciating the importance and interdependence of both elements.

*"The only Zen you find on the tops of mountains is the Zen you bring up there"*

*Robert M Pirsig – Zen and the Art of Motorcycle Maintenance*

# 11. AND FINALLY...WHERE IS ALL THE ZEN THEN?

I started this book by saying it wasn't about Zen – of course it is and isn't!

It was certainly never meant to be (and isn't) any sort of expert or definitive manual on the subject... actually, is it possible to produce anything definitive on a subject as 'large' and indefinable as Zen?

What I have attempted to do though, is 'throw' a few key messages and thoughts your way, messages from Pirsig and others, messages from my own life discoveries – pieces of my jigsaw.

In relation to Zen perhaps the main message from my perspective is that we all just simply need to keep our eyes and ears (and other senses) open to new possibilities. New ways of seeing what we take for granted. New ways to re-frame our world. I don't believe we can actually 'enforce' our learning, or that of others, we can only create environments that are conducive for it to occur.

> *"Find it and fix it just doesn't work!"*
>
> *"Just be present and put out the welcome mat for whatever arises"*
>
> *Jon Kabat-Zinn – 2013 Bangor University Mindfulness Conference*

It is at this point I have an image of a Zen Monk, kneeling on a long path made up of tiny white stones. The work he has been set is to pick up and clean each stone. An impossible and unending task and one that he will inevitably question - i.e. 'what is the point in this?' But one that may be the catalyst for some greater understanding at a deeper level. As a slight aside, how many of us have been at work (usually after a long formal meeting) and asked the same

Where is all the Zen then?

question!

Of course I am not suggesting that HR departments throughout the world send their staff out to clean stones! But what I am suggesting is that if people are given quality time out of their task or problem focused lives, and put into an environment where they can look at the same things in a different way, this will usually produce positive results.

Through the use of AI thinking and the application of the 5D cycle, the nature of conversations within organisations will inevitably change. And through this change people will start to see old problems in new ways – they will see solutions and they will be totally engaged with the journey they need to take in order to deliver on these solutions. All this being grounded on their own experiences (Discovery).

You may feel the link with Zen is tenuous. However, the increasing interest in mindfulness referred to earlier in this book is an indication of the meeting of traditional Western and Eastern ways of thinking (in this area and many others). The concept of being 'in the here and now' is the essence of both approaches (Zen and mindfulness), and although the focus on mindfulness still tends to be in relation to individual health benefits - as I have pointed out earlier, organisations are made up of individuals!

The Spring 2011 edition of the Ashridge Journal explores 'mindful leadership' and refers to the 'cognitive capacities required of knowledge workers in the modern economy'. The paper goes on to refer to findings coming out of the American Institute of Health, the University of Massachusetts, and the Mind and Body Medical Institute at Harvard University. These point to benefits in relation to:

> "We can make our minds so like still water that beings gather about us that they may see, it may be, their own images, and so live for a moment with a clearer, perhaps even with a fiercer life, because of our quiet"
>
> W.B. Yeats.

- o Reduced costs of staff absenteeism caused by illness, injury, stress
- o Improved cognitive function – including better concentration, memory, learning ability and creativity
- o Improved productivity and improved overall staff and business wellbeing
- o Reduced staff turnover and associated costs
- o Enhanced employer/employee and client relationships
- o Reduced health insurance premiums for the business

- A visible and tangible corporate responsibility stance
- Enhanced employee job satisfaction

Of course, as a good Psychologist friend of mine will constantly (and rightly) point out – there could be all sorts of other factors that may have impacted on these results. Making any sort of cast-iron conclusions in relation to the world of human behaviour is probably nigh on impossible. However, I, like all of us, can only go with what I experience in this world, slowly forming my own conclusions, slowly conducting my own little piece of research. Added to this I see and hear what others have said and written (some of which I have quoted in this book) – and use this as 'evidence' to support my world view.

But if there is one thing I can say with complete conviction and confidence it is that we all have our own world views. And that fact alone gives credence to AI and one of its main foundation stones – social constructionism.

So that's it, from just one guy who has struggled with all this 'stuff' over many years. Who has been looking for some meaning in many or all parts of his life. Who is actually quite critical in terms of the unending line of new management theories. Who has tried to keep an open mind to new possibilities. And... who thinks that an AI way of thinking and approach actually makes a lot of logical sense...

Have a great trip!

## Where is all the Zen then?

*Futile the talk that is bandied about, when many join in, each listening only to his own words or hearing only himself speaking in the words of his neighbour.*

*It is the same with books; for everyone will read out of the book only himself or will forcibly read himself into it, making the strangest amalgam.*

*Utterly futile, therefore, to endeavour by writing to change a man's inclination, the bent of his mind.*

*You will only succeed in confirming him in his opinions. Or, if he has none, drenching him with your own.*

*Goethe, "First Epistle"*

# References

## Books

'Appreciative Inquiry Handbook' by David L. Cooperrider, Diana Whitney and Jacqueline M. Stavros. Published by Crown Custom Publishing Inc and Berrett-Koehler Publishers Inc.

'The Thin Book of Appreciative Inquiry' by Sue Annis Hammond. Published by the Thin Book Publishing Co.

'Zen and the Art of Motorcycle Maintenance: An Inquiry into Values' by Robert Pirsig. Published by Bodley Head. Reprinted by permission of The Random House Group Limited (UK) and HarperCollins Publishers (USA)

'On Becoming a Person' by Carl R. Rogers. Published by Constable & Company Ltd.

## Papers

'When is Appreciative Inquiry Transformational? A Meta-Case Analysis' by Gervase R. Bushe. Faculty of Business Administration, Simon Fraser University.

'Evaluation of Appreciative Inquiry Interventions' by Martin Stellnberger. A thesis submitted to the Victoria University of Wellington. Victoria University of Wellington 2010.

'Why Does Affect Matter in Organizations?' by by Sigal G. Barsade and Donald E. Gibson. Academy of Management Perspectives.

'Mindful leadership: Exploring the value of a meditation practice' - The Ashridge Journal - Mindful leadership: Exploring the value of a meditation practice. Spring 2011.

## And all the others

I would also like to thank all the other authors and speakers who have subliminally informed my thinking and hence this book. I may not have named you but my thanks go out to you.

Roger and his XT500 in earlier years

## ABOUT THE AUTHOR

Roger Rowett lives in North Wales, UK with his family and his dog. He has found life challenging and difficult at times but has always been an observer, trying to learn, develop and improve. He has worked for a multitude of organisations who have also been trying to learn, develop and improve. This book is an attempt to share his learning, the most profound of which is 'we all have to find our own way'. And if that is true, AI has meaning.

If you would like to explore other people's views and ideas about this book, or share your own, there is a Facebook Page and LinkedIn group dedicated to this. Just search on the book title.

Printed in Great Britain
by Amazon